WEAPONS FOR
VICTORY

Memoirs of a Perfect Storm

REVISED EDITION

Dr. Sharon Arrindell

Cover Design: Minister Noel McDonald
Email: na.mcdonald@me.com

Dedication

I write this revised version of this book as a celebration of all the victories I have won in Jesus name, and dedicate it first and foremost to the Lover of my soul. It is also dedicated to my deceased parents Ira and Lena Ferguson who raised me well. To my children Jason Smith and Shanae Nicholas, my son-in-law Ian Nicholas II, daughter-in-law Cabrea, and grandchildren, Alex, Leilani, Caleb, and Myla, who are always at the forefront of every project I pursue. To my biological sister Joy Marshall who led me to the Lord at 10 years old, and all my family members who stood in the gap for me. I also dedicate this book to my friend Berneida Evans (Rosie) who helped me to get up when I was down for the count. Also, to my bishop and church family at Bethel Gospel Assembly in Harlem N.Y. I pray that all who will read this revised copy will gain courage for their own lives.

Preface

The Bible declares in 2 Corinthians 10:4 that, *"The weapons we fight with are not the weapons of this world. On the contrary, they have divine power to demolish strongholds."* The Christian is given automatic weapons, that when relinquished, are able to destroy everything in their path and lead the believer to ultimate victory. This book, by using Paul's description of the believer's fight and weaponry in Ephesians 6:10-18, will take the reader into the author's own journey, and reveal how God showed up as the covering needed on every terrain. The book is a biographical portrait of one who lived on the edge, stepped out on nothing, and exercised mustard seed faith. While this will be a study of the weaponry given to every believer in the fight for their lives, it will unveil the story of one believer's decision to muster all the strength needed to use these weapons and win. The Christian is in a fight for their soul, but God does not leave us to ourselves, but gets in the trenches with us, giving us the impetus to win. The spiritual battle we fight is a warfare of faith that must be fought to the bitter end, but we have the divine assurance that we will win if we don't give up (Galatians 6:9). Jesus, by shedding His blood has already triumphed over the enemy of our souls by disarming every evil force and influence, thus making us winners.

CONTENT

<u>Summary</u>
Prayer Changes Things

<u>The Journey Continues</u>

<u>Introduction</u>
<u>Gaining Strength for the Journey</u>
"Finally be strong in the Lord and in His mighty power".
Ephesians 6:10

As a counselor I have been given access to the emotional, mental, and spiritual world of others to help bring closure, healing and at times restoration of life. I have been given access to work in the secular and currently work in the Christian counseling venue. I recognize that the hand of God has been on my life since I started this colossal journey. About twelve years ago as I sat in front of my computer to compose this manuscript of my memoirs I realized that if this was going to bring healing and wholeness I would need to revisit some places on this journey that I have left untouched. Hence it has been a tug of war between me and God because there are some things I would rather have left unsaid. Thus, the book was kept sealed in my saved files for what seemed like a lifetime, before I was given a nudge by the Holy Spirit to reenter the pages and inscribe each word, with all dictates coming from the Master. The voice of the Holy

Spirit came in a whisper one early morning while visiting my family in California. As I prayed and pushed back the tears I was consumed with the fact that although some of the words and actions of the past will wreak judgment from those most righteous, the lyrics chosen will bring healing and wholeness to the masses. I prayed for God to take me by the hand and literally pen these pages with me, and I trusted Him to capture the attention of my audience who read and would gain strength for their own journey. As I looked to God for a title to this volume of memories, He reminded me about my many excursions through Ephesians 6:10-18 and how the believer needs to strategically embrace each "Weapon for Victory".

I can vividly remember as my ex-husband stepped up to the dirt floor podium in 1998, at a summer retreat that our family attended annually with New Horizons Ministries. He pronounced with great conviction that "you cannot have a new beginning until you come to the end of yourself". I honestly believe God gave him those words for himself that day. However, the words were also etched in my spirit, and when I was faced with the decision of having to start all over, I recognized that God had used him to speak words that would thrust me on the most difficult journey of my life. The question flooded my mind, "How do I get to the end of myself"? Paul, in Ephesians 6:10 recognized that exuberant strength would be needed to confront the enemy the believer would contend with. He, therefore, commanded that we *"be strong in the Lord"*, because there would be no other way to conquer and win. Without a doubt, I knew I would have to face the strongholds that were trying to infiltrate my life, and I could only do that with the help of the one I call Abba Father.

I grew up in a home where I was sheltered by parents, who although not perfect, set the atmosphere for a safe haven. They were married for 46 years before my dad passed away, and I remember their doors always being open to receive any and all who needed a secure refuge. Although they birthed only two biological children, Velma (V), Sharonette (Sharon), and Leary became products of the open door policy that their home represented. They were amazing, and although they had very little worldly possessions, they camouflaged by extending an abundance of love. I can remember as though it was yesterday, someone needing a place to stay and my mom uttering the all-consuming words, "we can't afford it". My dad always replied with great conviction "God will provide". What an awesome pair who always compensated for each other's short comings until their marriage was ended by death. They were my role model for marriage, so when all hell broke loose in my home, and I was faced with the advent of starting over, I felt no recourse, but to curl up in a corner and die. Self as I had known it had come to a screeching halt, and every crevice of my mind was filled with defeat. The enemy had come into my camp with all the forces of hell, and I felt too frail to fight.

My biological sister Joy, who is twelve years my senior, led me to the Lord at the age of ten. She was, and still is one of the most devoted Christian women I know, and I remember wanting to be just like her when I grew up, which drew me to ask her to lead me in the sinner's prayer that January day in 1970. As I reflect on this awesome woman of God I can honestly say that in all the time I've known her I have never seen her perform a wrong deed. Her motives have always been *"whatever is true, whatever is noble, whatever is right, whatever is pure, whatever is lovely, and whatever is admirable— if anything is excellent or praiseworthy — think about such things.*" (Philippians 4:8) I believe her thought life has been so entrenched in these words; they have produced a wholesome life to those looking on. I recall being reprimanded by our mother on several occasions, and while I always held a grudge, my sister Joy would always exhibit the utmost respect. Although our relationship has been somewhat distant while growing up, I have watched her from a distance and sincerely believe she has lived up to the meaning of her name.

I moved to New York almost immediately after that memorable introduction to my Lord and Savior, and at the age of sixteen my mind became consumed with worldly distractions. Although I became a rebel without a cause, I always prided myself on being okay with God, because I never put myself in a position of stepping outside of certain boundaries that I established. At eighteen years old I went on a vacation to Jamaica with my dad, and during that trip I was able to spend some time with my sister Joy. Her radiant smile and calming deportment quickly reminded me of who I was in God and that I needed to re-invest in my relationship with Him. I also met a young man on that trip.

Although we had grown up in Olivet Sunday School together, I always remembered him as the scrawny kid with the big ears that played the piano. That kid had grown into a handsome young man that would spend that entire vacation melting my heart. We spent every day of that trip together, as he took me to places in Jamaica that I had never been. Up until then I had only met young men who focused on the outward, but I felt he truly wanted to know who I was and he made every effort to do that. We were only eighteen, but found ourselves contemplating marriage. I wondered how this would last as I was living so many miles away in New York, but I never allowed this to cloud our times together. My dad, however, with all the wisdom he could muster, declared to me on the night before our return trip to New York that I was too young to be married and would have to finish my education before contemplating such things. The plane ride back was filled with tears, as I realized this relationship would not last and I would need to put my feelings for this young man on hold in hopes that I would meet him again one day. I made the mistake of not corresponding with him after a couple of letters, and two years later when I returned to Jamaica I learned he was engaged to be married. He visited our home in Jamaica while I was there, and his words made me comprehend that I had lost touch with him in more ways than one and I was devastated. Through the years I have often wondered what might have happened if I had thrown caution to the wind, disobeyed my dad and married that man.

I returned to New York and escaped that season of life by re-visiting the phase of my life that I so desperately wanted to change. I chose to care about nothing and no one including myself. In 1980 I experienced a fateful event that would crush my spirit and send me into a tailspin. 1Corinthians 10:13 states *"No temptation has overtaken you except what is common to mankind. And God is faithful; he will not let you be tempted beyond what you can bear. But when you are tempted, He will also provide a way out so that you can endure it"*. However, when I refused to accept the way of escape provided by God, and found out two months later that I was pregnant, everything changed. I was scared to death, but still continued on the lying path that I had so deviously created, allowing all my church cronies to think I was pure as the driven snow. I made the decision that I would tell no one, and kept that secret from everyone, even those close to me, like my best friend, with whom I had established a David and Jonathan relationship; along with others who I referred to as friends. I was embarrassed and afraid of what people would think, and how it would affect my parents and family who had raised me with strict moral values. On that most memorable day of my life I got on a bus, went to the hospital and aborted that child. It was the hardest decision I had ever made and one that I would have to live with for the rest of my life. Although many years have passed, I still find myself wondering at times what would have become of that child, and how life would have been different if I had resolved to take courage and do the right thing. I can still remember the sound of the machine used to help me commit pre-meditated murder that day. I was shattered and unable to sleep for months, and even years to come as I held on to the guilt and shame. At times I was consumed with suicidal thoughts, but was too afraid to act on them. I thought if I continued to party with my friends it would make me forget and give me a reason to keep living, so I became a party animal. It is my desire that in revealing this episode in my life I will inspire some teenager or young adult not to make this devastating mistake, but to grab hold of the way of escape provided by God; and if the escape choice is not made, then gain the courage to own the mistake knowing God will forgive.

I had grown accustomed to lying to my parents when I wanted to be with my friends, and have what I called "Big Fun". I can remember the night when this lifestyle would come to a screeching halt. It was New Year's Eve 1981 and I had just come from church where I played my hypocritical role as lead singer in the youth choir. My friends and I decided we were going to ring in the New Year at a house party. I vividly remember wearing a red strapless dress with a matching flower on the side of my hair (it was my Billy Holiday look). I camouflaged the outfit by wearing my winter coat over the dress, and once again lied to my parents that I was going to an all-night youth church event. I had become a pathological liar and did it without flinching. There were about nine of us cramped into a small Toyota Camry that night, on our way to ring in the New Year at a party. This had become a way of life for me as I lived my double life, being holier than thou on Sunday while, as the youth of today would say, "droppin it like it's hot" on Saturday nights. I was sitting in the back seat of the car on someone's lap, on that memorable night, when a car slammed into us. I call to mind being thrown from the car on to the sidewalk, and it felt like I literally heard God say "choose today who you are going to serve". I was in shock and didn't even realize where I was. However, I knew my life needed to change, and this was the setting God was using to do it. I vowed that night to serve God with all the passion I could muster, and although temptations came with all the forces of hell at times, I fought to keep my promise.

I stayed for endless hours in my bedroom reading the Word and praying like I had never done before. I cried out to God to forgive me, and He gave me verse after verse that spoke about Him being forgiving. The verses inscribed on my heart were *"Who is a God like you, who pardons sin and forgives the transgression of the remnant of His inheritance? You do not stay angry forever, but delight to show mercy. You will again have compassion on us; You will tread our sins underfoot and hurl all our iniquities into the depths of the sea".* (Micah 7:18-19) *"As far as the east is from the west, so far has He removed our transgressions from us"*. (Psalm 103:12) *Then I acknowledged my sin to You and did not cover up my iniquity. I said, "I will confess my transgressions to the LORD." And You forgave the guilt of my sin"*. (Psalm 32:5)

Focusing on those verses set me free and for years to come I would continue making the decision to serve God with a spirit of veracity, seeking to teach other young people to do the same.

Although God had healed me and given me the courage to start my life with Him all over, what was about to ensue was warfare like I had never known. Although I had turned my back on God for a season, I grew up in a Plymouth Brethren church where Sunday school lessons were taught with an importance on memorizing the Word of God. I call to mind Olivet Gospel Hall in Jamaica W.I. and Grace Gospel Chapel in Harlem New York, and the men and women of God who taught me the Word with conviction. Prizes were often presented to those who memorized the most scriptures, and even though I was living my double life I managed to memorize scripture on a daily basis (hoping to receive one of the great prizes). Those were fun years and memorization always came easy to me. Sunday school teachers and even elders in those churches often commented on how amazing it was that I could not only memorize verses, but at times entire chapters of the Bible.

Years later, when the rubber hit the road and these scriptures had to be fleshed out, I was dumb struck and paralyzed in my thoughts. I had come to a road block in my life and although the detour signs were there, like the Israelites, I was blinded by the size of the giants in my promised land. Although the weapons of my warfare were built into the very fabric of my being, all I saw was a line drawn in the sand that I could not cross because I quaked in my boots with fear.

Isaiah 54:17 explains, *"No weapon forged against you will prevail, and you will refute every tongue that accuses you. This is the heritage of the servants of the Lord, and this is their vindication from Me, declares the Lord."* I knew this scripture well and had quoted it many times in the past, but now I had to breathe it and the thought evaporated everything within me. A tornado had hit and wiped out every dream and promise in its path. I felt like I had been punched in the chest and was gasping for air with no assistance in sight. All my defenses were down and I was vulnerable to the attacks of Satan and his cohorts. I had a myriad of decisions to make about what to do next, but I was stuck in a fetal position on the floor. Although I knew I needed to *"forget those things that were behind so I could press towards what was ahead"* (Philippians 3:13), there was a force holding me in that position and I became hostage to it. Family and friends stepped in, but I needed the life line that only God could give, and this would only manifest itself when I came to the end of myself.

Although I rebelled against them a lot, my parents had always made life seem somewhat easy, and at times I even thought we were wealthy, because we never seemed to lack anything. Although they loved me and tried to protect me, their protection did not prepare me for what I was about to face in the arena of life. My dad was always extremely protective; I can even remember being given the alternative of either not going to my High School prom or going with him as my escort. I chose the latter and although embarrassed at first, I managed to have a good time with the man who raised me and taught me everything I knew about the male species. When he and my mom migrated to the U.S. they made it possible for me to join them a short while later. I remember him always being at every event during my school days, because he always ensured that I attended school in the vicinity of his workplace. I always looked forward with anticipation to, what I will refer to as our Friday evening rendezvous, when he would pick me up from school and take me to dinner at his favorite Chinese restaurant in Harlem N.Y. He opened my door, pulled out my chair and offered all the courtesy of a gentleman. When I asked why he did all this he would respond, "This is what you must seek when looking for the right person to marry". Although I thought it humorous and old fashioned at the time, I recognized years later that he wanted only the best for me, hence, the reason for his at times over protective nature.

Chapter 1

The Calm before the Storm

"Put on the full armor of God so that you can take your stand against the devil's schemes." Ephesians 6:11

It was as a result of my daddy's teaching that I met and married who I thought was the most incredible person. As I journey back in time I remember our meeting very well. It was a singles retreat in the early portion of 1989, with the new church I started attending; Bethel Gospel Assembly, also in Harlem N.Y. I joined that church in 1987, when I felt the leading of God, after spending most of my life in the teaching of the Brethren traditions. This was a massive move, but one I felt God impressing on me for a while. Thus, I looked forward to these singles excursions that always proved beneficial in me learning how to live single and Godly. As I got on the bus, I proceeded to sit with my friend. As we talked and laughed preparing for the trip, I heard a calm voice come from behind beckoning her to "move because she was in his seat". Although at the time I thought this was the most preposterous request I had ever heard, she exited the seat without question, beginning what would become a whirlwind romance that would eventually lead to marriage. I call to mind praying for God to reveal who I would marry by allowing me to encounter a man after His heart. Thus, I recognized this person immediately because he seemed to love the Lord with a force I had never encountered before.

Our courtship was filled with unusual events. A simple subway ride would spiral into my date managing to find someone (most times derelicts who had the worse stench I ever encountered), to whom he could minister and at times win to the Lord. I remember accompanying him to one of his many hospital visits. While waiting in the car he returned without the shirt on his back, stating he gave it to someone who needed it more than he did. I was amazed at how dedicated he was to reaching the lost for Christ, and in retrospect this is how he managed to win my heart. Love was in the air and six months after that memorable singles retreat we were engaged to be married. I had prayed for a husband that God would call a man after His heart, and I believed with everything in me that I had found that person. What my daddy had instilled in me about what to seek in a man had been fleshed out and I felt undeserving of the blessing. We immediately sought pre-marital counseling from the then associate pastor of our church, and current bishop of Bethel Gospel Assembly, Carlton Brown, and he left no stone unturned in explaining to us the good, bad and ugly of marriage. At the end of those sessions we felt that God had used him to equip us for whatever we would face on this journey called marriage. Our final session was with the late Bishop Ezra Williams, and he put the icing on the cake, when he explained that in putting two people together from different backgrounds stress would ensue, hence making marriage one of the most stressful relationships to be built by Almighty God. He countered that statement by invoking the fact that when God is the unseen guest in every situation of that marriage, the couple is given the ability to live a lifetime together. We had been given all the ammunition to fulfill God's plan and live together till death, but we knew we had to keep God in the midst to make that a reality. God had used two awesome men to equip us with strength for this marital journey and we felt ready.

We were married December 23rd 1989. It was my 30th birthday and one of the coldest December days New York had experienced in a very long time. I remember the weather forecast claiming the wind chill factor to be below zero. However, like most couples in love and destined for a future, our hearts were warm with love and excitement at the advent of a future together. Family members came from the warmth of Jamaica and Florida just to share in our day. It made our hearts glad to see the outpouring of love. There were over two hundred guests in attendance, all decked in their finest attire for what many referred to as the wedding of the decade. I remember walking down the aisle on the arm of my dad, who explained on that final journey of singlehood, how proud he was of the choice I had made in a husband. It was a beautiful day, and although it was chilling cold outside, all hearts were warm as they waited for us to declare our love before God and all in attendance. Although it had been years since I sang a solo, I belted out a song from my heart to the one I thought would be my life partner. The words of the song went like this:

"Make us one with one another one with Thee,

Make a love so strong between us that the world will clearly see,

That however great the problem we soon will overcome,

Cause we're anchored in the Father and walking with the Son".

Make us one with one another one with Thee,

Help us feel each other's feelings and share each other's needs,

Then our lives will bear the witness of Jesus glorified,

And the world will know you sent Him and He gives eternal life,

Make us one heart, one mind, one hope, our hope is in You.

Those words are engraved in my memory for life, and as I counsel countless couples today, who are about to take this crucial step, I often remind them that their marriage will only make it if they're anchored in the Father and walking with the Son. Although not a veteran, my ex-husband was decked in civil war military attire for our wedding. I believe he supernaturally knew this would be warfare like he had never known.

We had a beautiful reception following our ceremony on a stationary boat on the Jersey side of the Hudson River. This had become our favorite restaurant while dating and we decided it would be perfect for our day. People talked about how cold it was on the boat, but like most couples in love we were numb to the cold and excited about what God was about to do in bringing us and our families together. We spent our honeymoon in Jamaica at a beautiful hotel in Ocho Rios, and it amazes me that I can remember to this day the peace that flooded my mind, because I thought God had brought someone into my life that loved Him more than he loved me. I thought this would be the glue that would make this a lifetime union. I thought we were the epitome of what marriage should be, and although I knew we would face struggles, I also knew we would make it through anything as long as our armor was in place. I was on the trip of my life and no matter what the enemy brought our way; I was in it for life because my Bible told me love was patient, kind, and longsuffering (1 Corinthians 13:4-8), a scripture that has the mantra when counseling couples.

The honeymoon was over and we were now faced with the advent of living together till death us do part. An apartment was unaffordable at first, but my dad the awesome giver he was, built an addition to his home so we could live there for a season. What was supposed to be a six month stay turned into two years, as we struggled to become financially well enough to make our exit into our own home. In February of 1991, at what I thought was an ordinary doctor's visit I learned I was pregnant, and unusual sickness overcame me almost immediately. What was supposed to be the most exciting time of my life became torture. The enemy sometimes troubled my mind by telling me it was payback for aborting my first child. God however, constantly reminded me that He was large and in charge and Satan was a liar who would only have the upper hand if I allowed him. Although everyone said the sickness would only last a short time, it went on for months and I was forced to resign my job. I was sick for the entire nine months of my pregnancy and at times had to be fed intravenously; hence, I lost twenty six pounds. I looked forward with anticipation to the birth of my first child and gave birth to a beautiful baby girl on November 20, 1991. She had a strong expression on her face from birth and we named her Shanae (God is gracious) Brianna (strong). She became our pride and joy as we immediately invested time praying and reading with her every day. She was the apple of her daddy's eyes and would change our lives forever.

My ex-husband was the priest of our home and never missed a moment in spending time with the Lover of his soul. I would wake up every morning to him on his face crying out to God as he started his day. At times it was annoying, as my former church culture had always been one of silence. Thus, I was always used to my mornings with the Lord being quiet and at times uneventful. However, I grew accustomed to these mornings of outpouring to God and looked forward with great anticipation to what I chose to call "our family altar".

Our marriage was consumed with ministry as my ex-husband continued to do street evangelism in Mount Morris Park across the street from our church every Saturday. It was in that park that I believe I learned how to rescue the perishing, and care for the dying, the first of whom was a young woman on a park bench, where she had spent the night. The man I married never missed a beat in seeking to win souls for Christ especially those who were downcast and down trodden. He was a David of his generation and carried out every task with a big grin on his face. He was very instrumental in a men's shelter in Harlem as well, and the men revered him as friend and mentor. We also served in the couple's ministry and taught Sunday school every Sunday. What a pair we were, and although the tasks were tedious at times, I vowed to be helper, companion, and friend till death. He was ordained a deacon and church leader shortly after our marriage, and although I recognized this was yet a higher call to service, I was in it for the long haul. I remember having to give a short speech on the day of his ordination, and quaked in my boots, because my former church culture, which prohibited women from speaking in the presence of men, was still engrained in every part of who I was. I managed to get through my longest five minutes of public speaking, promising to be a wife that would work beside my husband to build up God's kingdom, hoping to never have to speak in the pulpit again.

I was involved in New Horizons Ministries prior to marrying my ex-husband. This non-profit ministry, by using the medium of retreats and summer camps, made mega investments in changing the lives of teenagers and young adults throughout the metropolitan area. It was also very instrumental in me re-dedicating my life to the Lord, and my spiritual growth thereafter. I can recall my first encounter with the ministry in 1983. The keynote speaker was a grey haired man named Ernie Wilson. I remember thinking why would they choose such an old man to reach young people, but it wasn't long before I recognized he was the perfect man for the job. My life was changed after that unforgettable first experience with this ministry, and I vowed to give back in any way possible. I had since become counselor, speaker, teacher and planner for this awesome work, hence my family followed suit and the ministry became an integral part of our lives.

Bethel Gospel assembly was and still is a Missions church and we knew at some juncture we would be called to either short term or full-time service. My ex-husband had gone on short term mission trips, but I had always stayed behind. However, on a special night in 1991 when our daughter was still a baby we were called into the office of the then Missions director Dr. Ruth Onuque, and I knew in my heart God was about to do something amazing. She asked if we would give up our lives in America and move to South Africa to facilitate a new school that Bethel was about to launch, and my mouth hung open. My ex-husband had worked with children, and although I had taught in the Sunday school department, and with New Horizons for years I wondered what this would mean for our family. We felt honored and afraid at the same time, but answered yes to the call. About one week later he received a phone call from Dr. Onuque, as he often did, beckoning him to come to her home. Upon his return I saw a look on his face that I had never seen before, and his speech was slurred as he proceeded to tell me he was HIV positive.

At that time this disease was taking lives like nothing I had ever seen, thus I thought this would probably kill him. However, in retrospect, God had prepared me in the week prior when I read in Essence Magazine about Magic Johnson's revelation to the world that he was HIV positive. I remember wondering, as I read an article written by Cookie Johnson, what my response would be if my husband gave me that news; and here I was being exposed to the news I wondered about. I was bare feet and sitting on the bed at the time, and all I could think about doing was running until I couldn't run anymore. I took off running bare feet down our street in the Bronx, with him chasing behind me apologizing and pleading with me not to end our marriage. Leaving the marriage was the farthest thing from my mind, but I was traumatized and unable to think straight and running seemed to cushion the blow. That was a pivotal point in our marriage, and I made the decision to fast and pray for fifty days; something I had never done before. God revealed to me during those days that *"this sickness was not unto death but to bring Him glory"*. (John 11:4)

Suddenly, I didn't recognize the person I married, because I believe his faith in God was shaken during this crucial time. I would wake up to him crying out to God to reverse the verdict and allow him to live through this life threatening disease, which had already taken the lives of so many people. This demon had entered our lives and we became victims, but I continued to pray wondering how and when this would somehow bring God glory. This was an all-consuming season that put a big dent in our marriage, as I watched this powerful man of God shake at times in fear.

In Ephesians 6:11 Paul beckons the believer to put on our full spiritual armor to fight against Satan's evil schemes. However, I believe it was at this juncture in our marriage that his armor produced its first crack. We made the decision not to have any more children, because we didn't quite understand this disease and what it would mean for them. However, God had another plan and when my daughter was only thirteen months old I found myself pregnant once again. The pregnancy was a repeat performance of sickness, compounded by the fear and uncertainty for the health of the child in my womb. I remember attending church and being told by respected and revered church folks that we were wrong for allowing this pregnancy. At times I just felt lost in the shuffle of Christianity, wondering if I stood alone in my faith. However, I gave birth to a beautiful baby boy, who I knew from birth, would bring joy and healing into our home with his peaceful presence. He was born on October 30, 1993 and I understood immediately that this boy would be a healer and was definitely a gift from God; hence we named him Jason (healer) Nathaniel (gift from God). The doctors pronounced him healthy and I rejoiced in my spirit. When I looked in my baby's face all I saw was the hand of God and I felt unexplainable peace.

Chapter 2

The Storm is Passing Over

"For our struggle is not against flesh and blood, but against the rulers, against the authorities, against the powers of this dark world and against the spiritual forces of evil in the heavenly realms". Ephesians 6:12

Prior to the birth of our son God opened the door for a job for my ex-husband. The job was in Rockland County New York, which was forty five minutes away from our home in the Bronx. We set out to find an apartment and found one almost immediately. It was a two bedroom apartment in the town of Spring Valley, and in hindsight the building somehow reminded me of the Bronx. We moved to Rockland County, to make, what we thought would be a better life for ourselves and our children. I was a stay at home mom who had put her dreams on hold to raise her children and I enjoyed more than anything teaching them how to read, write, and most importantly how to live for the Lord. This was the most important job I have ever encountered to date, as I had the lives of two little people in the palm of my hands. I was determined to train them in the way they should go, remembering the

Biblical promise that *"they would not depart when they got older.* (Proverbs 22:6) This was a challenging task, but one that I was prepared to tackle and win. My children were entrusted to me as a precious gift from God, and I was grateful to Him for the opportunity to be their care giver. The work was great, but I knew the rewards would be even greater. I recognized at this juncture that I was one of few women who had made the choice to stay home with their children during the formative years of their life, but I had made the decision, and was willing to give it my very best.

We continued to commute forty five minutes to an hour back and forth to the Bronx, in an effort to spend time with our family, but as a result of a near fatal accident, I refused to get behind the wheel of the car. The accident happened in 1987 and landed me in a hospital bed for six days. This accident left me deathly afraid of getting behind the wheel. However, I knew in my heart that God had moved us to Rockland to release me from that fear. It was a summer afternoon and I decided this would be the day I would venture to drive again. I was terrified and felt like a new driver, but I was ready. I asked my ex-husband to sit alongside me for support, but I couldn't stop my legs from shaking. He chuckled as I tried to catch my bearings and I can remember as if it was yesterday the anger that came over me out of nowhere, as I spontaneously took my hand from the steering wheel balled up my fist and punched him right in the mouth. In hindsight, I believe this was lingering anger from all our marriage, had and continued to endure. I surprised my own self with that reaction, and realized I had startled him as well. He silently removed himself from the vehicle, as I proceeded to re-teach myself how to drive. Like many other things I would have to tackle I did it alone and afraid. I drove alone for hours that day, recognizing I would have to go back home and apologize for what I had done. Although the apology was not received immediately, it was eventually. Driving a car, though second nature for many had become a major achievement for me, and I thanked God every day for getting me over that hurdle. In 1995 we moved from our two bedroom apartment to a townhouse that we would rent, hoping to one day purchase it as our home. In September of that same year I lost my dad and best friend, and though he was sick for a while, I missed him tremendously. His voice of love and encouragement would be remembered forever in the recesses of my mind.

In 1996 we had an encounter with a memorable pastor from Pittsburgh named. She recognized immediately when we went to the altar for prayer that my ex-husband was encountering some physical difficulties, and healing was needed. She invited us to spend some time with her in Pittsburgh and we accepted the invitation as a call, to not only physical healing, but rekindling in our marriage. Prior to going on that memorable trip, I spoke to God about speaking in tongues, and desiring that manifestation of His Spirit. I had been saved for a long time and wondered at times if the gift of tongues really existed today, because I had never encountered it. While on that fifty-day consecration I asked God to empower me with this gift. On that unforgettable trip the pastor invited me to spend some time in the church basement to pray. What a crucial moment it was, in that while having a casual conversation and praying, my mouth opened and I had no control over what was coming out. This was the prayer language I asked God to bless me with, and my Christian walk would never be the same. As stated previously, I grew up in a Plymouth

Brethren church, and while the Biblical teaching I received was second to none, the gift of tongues was eliminated and I always thought it was not for this age. I returned to N.Y. knowing there was a change that God had indelibly made, and I felt joy. When my ex-husband went to the doctor the prognosis registered healing on the horizon. I saw characteristics of God in the atmosphere that I was never privy to prior to my supernatural experience in that Pittsburg church basement. Though the circumstances that brought us to a turning point in our marriage had not drastically changed, I had deepened my relationship with the Lover of my soul, and felt ready for front line ministry. I realized immediately that the stage was set for WAR like I had never known and I braced myself for whatever would come next. I knew that if God allowed it He had the power to see me through it. Although I had almost jeopardized my relationship with Him as a stubborn rebellious teenager, He had compassionately forgiven my indiscretions and graciously placed me in the same category with Job, entrusting me to serve Him even when stripped of everything that I held near and dear.

It was September 1999 when Hurricane Floyd hit Rockland County N.Y. and a devastating shock for my family. I had just retrieved my children from the school bus and the rain was pouring like I had never seen before. Like any other day the children were relaxed in the basement watching television while I worked in my sewing room as I normally did. However, this would prove to be no ordinary day as I watched the rain through the huge glass doors of the basement. The phone rang, and it was my sister in law inquiring about our safety. As I proceeded to inform her that we were safe, I walked to the glass doors and pressed my bare feet against the carpet. The water was coming in under the carpet at a rapid pace. I coerced my children to go up the stairs, while I tried to salvage as many things as I could, recognizing that the water had now proceeded up the glass door and was almost to the top. In my ignorance, I wondered what would happen once the water got to the top. Before I could get anything in my hands I heard a crashing sound that I will never forget, as I watched the door cave right into the house and listened as the roaring of the water made me cringe. I froze for a moment in shock when all I could hear was my daughter screaming "mommy run". In retrospect I believe her scream saved my life on that haunting day, and I did just as she said, I grabbed my children and ran through the muddy water making my way to my neighbor's house for shelter. While I sat in their kitchen I could hear the same crashing sound coming through their basement, realizing that the entire neighborhood was under attack and all we could do was pray and wait for the storm to subside. My ex-husband was not home when the storm hit, but I could hear him screaming our names from around the corner as he approached the house that night, realizing this was no ordinary night.

As we ventured back to our home and sat on the basement stairs, all I remember hearing the man I called husband say with extreme regret was, "we have lost everything" and right behind those words came his soft voice proclaiming, "I am done with God". I couldn't believe what my ears were hearing. All he could see was the glass half empty while I was seeing it half full. God had spared my life and the life of my children, and although things looked dim and I couldn't see the handwriting on the wall, I knew God had a perfect plan. The man I married however, had changed right before my eyes. His passion for God that had won my heart ten years earlier, had turned into something that I had never seen before. I realized the enemy had infiltrated the heart of the man I referred to as husband, lover and friend. I had not only lost a house and things that were replaceable, but I had also lost the glue that held our family together; the priest of our home. There was hollowness in my heart and for the first time since we got married I was uncertain if this would be "till death us do part". I searched every scripture that promised release from fear, seeking to find solace in this moment, but I was frozen in time.

Our home was destroyed in more ways than one on that haunting day, and we woke up the next morning realizing we had nowhere to live. We were on the brink of being homeless, but God sent a safety net when my friend Rosie and her husband Charles offered the use of the lower floor of their home, for what seemed like the longest season of my life. We had gone from a townhouse with four bedrooms, to a two room lower floor apartment in a matter of minutes, but I held fast to the scripture that declared, *"The glory of this latter house shall be greater than of the former, saith the LORD of hosts: and in this place will I give peace, saith the LORD of hosts."* (Haggai 2:9) No matter how hard I tried, my peace had been threatened and I was in a warzone with the enemy of my soul. He had affirmed war and I have to admit, in retrospect, I was not ready for what was about to ensue. I let my guard down and Satan and his cronies took up residence in my home and I felt crushed. The war had begun, I had signed up for frontline duty and I was being hit from every direction. My ex-husband's complete armor was about to fall off, wreaking havoc for three unsuspecting victims. Regardless of how this moment felt, God had allowed it and I knew He would be with me to the finish. Questions bombarded my mind, I questioned God, and I questioned myself. In hindsight, I remember thinking I was being stripped of everything, and it almost felt like I was having an outer body experience. I thought this couldn't really be happening to me because I had always prayed and believed God for everything. However, God wanted to teach me something about His awesome power, and He wanted my undivided attention to do it.

Prior to the storm erupting in our home I registered for a course called Purity with Purpose that was being offered to the women in my church. The storm hit when we were three weeks into the course making every lesson that much more intense, as God was dealing with me each week. I recall realizing that God was using this class to bring me into a greater understanding of Him and what He had in store for my future. I found out in that class that my name meant "vision of beauty, grace and love", and realized this was meant especially for that inner person God expected me to be, I determined in my mind to live up to the meaning of my name. We went through several seasons of prayer and fasting during that course, culminating with a soul tie burning ceremony. I was always very leery about these types of rituals, but I also knew there were some things in my life that I just needed to be rid of once and for all. It took me back to several events that I thought I had already been healed from. However, this was the night that I would truly shed the guilt of an abortion that took place so many years prior. I became drunk in the spirit that night and I could hardly see to drive home. I felt drained, but it was a great feeling. After about 12-15 weeks of intense reevaluation of self, the class concluded in December 1999, with a graduation which included a ceremony ring and a prophetic word for each graduate. As I listened to all the exciting prophecies that came forth for my fellow graduates, I was excited to hear what God had to say to me, all dressed in white and seemingly ready for anything. I thought I had been through a lot and whatever would come next I would be armed and ready. As I stood in the pulpit that day declaring and decreeing all that I believed God had in store for my future, the prophet placed her hand on my head and although she said many things, all I could hear was her voice pronouncing "you will be wounded so you can help the wounded". Those words would forever be engraved in my memory, as I knew when I stepped off that stage that something enormous was about to follow.

My ex-husband woke up one April morning in 2000 and told me he would be leaving for a short while so he could think about some things. When I asked where he was going he refused to tell me. As he walked out the door I remember thinking he may not return, however, I proceeded to pray. It was the most confusing prayer I had ever echoed because I wasn't sure what I should pray, so most of the time was spent groaning. I was weak, but God remained strong and Romans 8:26 was about to be fleshed out in my life, *"The Spirit helps us in our weakness. We do not know what we ought to pray for, but the Spirit Himself intercedes for us with groans that words cannot express"*. He returned from his mysterious trip looking like he had encountered Satan face to face and was no longer equipped to fight. His face was dark, and he had even grown a small beard that he didn't have when he left a few days earlier. As I sat on the pull out sofa, that had now become a bed for us, I remember him saying "I can't do this anymore, I'm out". Those were the most riveting words I had heard since the day we married, and I felt my lips shaking as I asked the all consuming question "what do you mean", to which I already knew the answer. Sometimes as I try to take inventory of that crucial night, I recognize the enemy had infiltrated his mind some time before, but I was in denial refusing to believe. I recall however, a Sunday afternoon in March 2000 when we had just returned from church. He dressed the children for the park, and when asked if I wanted to join them I replied that I was tired and was just going to take a nap. While lying on the couch I received a phone call from an unfamiliar male voice telling me my husband had taken his wife to the park some hours ago and had not returned. This, I believe was the beginning of the end, because it was the start of the adulterous relationship that would be the reason for my already festering marriage to disintegrate.

The devil plotted to destroy our home and was determined to leave no survivors. Although my armor was available with all parts intact, I needed to wake up and strategically put each part in place piece by piece, determined to stand in this warzone and win. When Paul wrote the book of Ephesians he was in prison on behalf of Christ. He yearned for God's people to go forward in faith, seeking to live lives commendable of the Lord Jesus Christ. This journey would require Spiritual Warfare at its best, and armor befitting a champion. Paul had an up close and personal view of the protective covering worn by the Roman soldiers of his day. Thus, he used each piece in Ephesians chapter 6 as exemplary of what the believer would need to win in the battle against the principalities and powers to be faced. In verse 12 Paul recognized, from all he had gone through, that he was in a war, and it wasn't against tangible opponents that he could see and touch, but against unseen, but deadly powers. The devil will work tirelessly to demolish what God builds; therefore, the believer requires complete armor. My desire was to live a serene life with minimal worries. However, I was in a battle, and I needed to know the prevailing strength of my enemy. I needed one central ingredient to fight, and that was the power of Almighty God. Only He could make me strong, and I had to remain in the Vine, because without Him I could not do anything. (John 15:1-5)

As I listened to the man of my dreams tell me how unhappy he was, using that as his excuse for making his exit, I felt consumed by a feeling I can't remember ever having. For the first time in my life I can honestly say I felt hate for the person I had spent years loving. How could this be? I wondered, but the answer was clear almost immediately, as I realized the man I fell in love with was filled with the Spirit of God, and this person was filled with a spirit I had only seen in people I normally kept at a distance. It was a heart wrenching and lonely moment. In that instant I wanted to just go to sleep, hoping I would wake up and it would all be a very bad dream. I said absolutely nothing in response to his decision, as I wasn't quite sure what would happen next. Everything became a blur and I was speechless. I had often read and heard about separation and divorce, but had never seen it up close and personal, so I had no idea what to say or do. My life was consumed with my husband and children. I was in it for better or worse, deciding that the only thing that would separate us was death. In retrospect this was a death of the spiritual kind, which I thought was even harder because the person was still physically very much alive. Questions flooded my mind as I wondered what I had done wrong. How could I fix this? Where was God? How could He allow this to happen? My body became limp and I sobbed as I slithered down the wall of the kitchen and ended up on the floor. I landed in a fetal position and it seemed like I re-visited that position over and over for at least two years. Although I masked being healed, wholeness seemed unattainable.

My friend Rosie who became a mother to me in so many ways, watched as I toiled through this journey. While only about 4 feet 10 inches tall, she exhibited mammoth strength, when at times she was able to demonstrate the tough love I needed to sustain me. She had a front row seat to my drama, and sometimes she exercised great wisdom in just listening without uttering a word. I believe she missed her calling and would have made an excellent counselor. I have committed to memory the instrumental moment when God used this woman to get me from the fetal position, that had become my comfort, and back to the reality that *"I could do all things through Christ who gives me strength"*. (Philippians 4:13) She came down the stairs as she normally did when she felt in her spirit that I needed her. I was in my favorite position on the floor, sobbing uncontrollable while my six-year old son watched in silence and my eight-year old daughter pleaded with me to get up because she needed me to take care of her and her brother. Rosie stood above me; at the time seeming like ten feet tall, she pointed her finger and shook her head while explaining that I had two choices; life or death, and she would not allow me to die on her watch. She grabbed my children and went back up the stairs as quickly as she came down, without even looking back for my reaction. I was alone in the room and as I slowly rose to my feet I looked in the mirror and did not recognize the person looking back. I had become a prisoner of war with only "One Person" who could set me free.

My children started asking questions, especially my daughter as she was the oldest and extremely vocal. All I can remember saying is we needed to pray for their dad and so we did. Our family devotion time became crucial, and we never forgot to pray for their dad. My daughter's prayer life at eight years old was unbelievable. She was filled with God's Spirit and would proceed, on every occasion, to pray for God to put back the piece of our family puzzle that was now missing. She brought tears to my eyes every time, because I knew there was a possibility that wouldn't happen. God gives us choices and her dad had decided to make the wrong one. I didn't want her to give up on God, or hate her father, so I needed wisdom to explain this to her and her brother. How do you explain this to an eight-year old and six-year old? All I could do was pray and ask God for the strength and the words to do it. Psalm 34:18 says, *"The Lord is close to the broken hearted and saves those who are crushed in spirit"*, and this was about to be reality in my life and the life of my children.

Though living in Rockland County was what we had become familiar with, I was drowning and needed a change in my surroundings. The memories were consuming me and I asked my brother and his wife if we could stay in their home for a short while, and he said yes. I immediately proceeded to pack as much as I could into the car. Although the journey was only a forty five minute drive, it required going through Bear Mountain, which had always been a terrifying drive, as a result of my previous bout with learning to drive again, even when someone else was the driver. In the midst of packing, my ex-husband showed up and just stood in the driveway watching me pack. In my heart I hoped he would say put everything back in the house and let's try to make this work. However, he just watched in silence as I drove away with our children in the back seat. I watched him in the rear view mirror and wondered what, if anything was going through his mind. It was the middle of the night as I drove through the mountain to get to their house, and although I was afraid I knew this was something I had to do to keep my sanity. I was even willing to sleep on the floor if I had to. My brother opened his home to us, and because I didn't want my children to change yet another school I commuted each day, to work in my store and to bring them to school. I was in constant prayer all the time, even when my prayers, at times, had no words.

While staying with my brother my ex-husband called almost every day asking when, or if, we would be returning to Rockland County. His voice was so sincere when he told me he wanted to give our marriage another chance. I was desperate to hear those words and decided to seriously think about putting our family back together. I knew God hated divorce, because He said it in his Word, and therefore, always made room for reconciliation even amidst adultery. He told me he would search for an affordable apartment, and proceeded to do just that. I was elated at the thought of my marriage being reconciled, but I was also terrified of the unknown. I was about to re-acquaint myself with someone who had become a stranger to me, but I was willing to make the sacrifice for my children. In all honesty I had never stopped loving my husband and I looked forward to some appearance of normalcy for our home. He finally found a place, and although it was in the backwoods of a town called Haverstraw that was very unfamiliar, I was willing to move, in an effort to get my home back. This was a desperate feat on both our parts as it was obvious that things had drastically changed between us. My self esteem was as low as it could get, as I fought daily to compete with a foe I had never met. When I looked in the mirror I saw ugly, never feeling good enough or pretty enough to be with this man, or compete with the one his eyes now favored. My lengthy strong hair had always been a part of me that I treasured, nevertheless the stress was mounting and I began to lose even that. At one point as I ran the comb through my hair I would watch it fall out in clumps. My Bible said I was *fearfully and wonderfully made* (Psalm 139), but I reckoned with the enemy of my soul who told me the opposite and I chose to believe the lie.

This move proved to be an exercise in futility, as it was obvious from his late night rendezvous and verbal discontent that the marriage was over in my ex-husband's mind. I recall a memorable night as in his usual soft tone, he told me everything he thought was wrong with me. I was angrier than I had ever been and as he walked out the door, with his back towards me, I held the snow shovel over my head in an effort to hit him as hard as I could. I had lost all sense of who I was and what I stood for. As I was about to bring that shovel down on his head I could see my children in my peripheral vision crouching in a corner in fear. I slowly put the shovel down and asked this man to leave our home for the last time. I felt in my spirit that this was the last straw for all of us, and although I still couldn't envision life without him I had to let go and truly realize that God was enough.

My daughter became ill after that and I attributed it to the fact that she had internalized so much it was manifesting itself in her body. I would get home in time to get her and her brother off the school bus and she would exit the bus with her shoes in her hands. Her feet and hands would be swollen as she cried in pain. She said it felt like pins and needles. At night she would cry endlessly as I rocked her in my arms and prayed. I had no idea what to do as the symptoms were not constant and only occurred when she thought about missing her dad. I remember her exhibiting excruciating pain one night that was accompanied by a high fever. When her dad came and held her in his arms the symptoms just seemed to disappear as quickly as they came. Although I recognized this was a stress related illness I also knew she could not continue like this, so I took her to the doctor who recommended complete testing to diagnose the problem. I watched as they proceeded to poke and prod taking and testing all the blood they could. They finally gave a diagnosis of juvenile arthritis and prescribed medication. I prayed that night for God to supernaturally heal my daughter. That was the first and last time I gave my daughter her medicine, as she never exhibited that type of pain ever again after that night. God is amazing, as Shanae would go forward to become a great praise dancer and do so many other awesome things that required the movement of her limbs.

Prior to that unforgettable storm that swept through our home leaving us dumb struck, I had decided, after years of designing and making beautiful bridal and evening gowns for people, to move this craft out of my basement and into a store. My dad had given me two middle names, Colleen Decadia that I usually ignored, however, when it came time to name the store I called it Decadia's Evening and Bridal. I tirelessly used my talent as a seamstress to create custom made bridal and evening dresses. The original plan was for my ex-husband to pay the bills until the store could pay for itself, but when the rug was pulled out from under me I found myself using every means at my disposal to keep this store afloat. I would wake up every morning, get dressed, with my children at my side, in an effort to get to the store by 4 am, to be ready to greet customers and keep the store from going under. That was an amazing exploit, but God was covering me as I prayed endlessly about what to do next. Although the store had always been a dream, it had now become a nightmare and I was physically, emotionally and mentally exhausted. After many months of trying to keep the store from going belly up, I made the hard decision to close the doors not knowing what I would do next, or how I would make it financially. I suppose most of the people who knew me and were observing this episode of my life, must have thought I was crazy. Although I was confused and unsure, I knew God was carrying me, and if I just closed my eyes I would feel safe in His arms. When friends and loved ones questioned, all I could say was I am in a "Perfect Storm" waiting to get to shore. Although it felt like a rollercoaster ride and I wanted to get off, in the back of my mind I knew God had a plan and He gave me a rhema word in Jeremiah 29:11, *"For I know the plans I have for you, declares the Lord, plans to prosper you and not to harm you, plans to give you hope and a future"*. The plan was unclear, but I knew God would never go back on His Word so I tried to remain still.

Chapter 3

Standing my Ground

"Therefore put on the full armor of God, so that when the day of evil comes, you may be able to stand your ground, and after you have done everything, to stand".
Ephesians 6:13

Subsequent to closing the store I proceeded to locate a job that would provide for my children and me. I was a novice about divorce and didn't quite understand the role of the court system. Thoughts of going to court to fight for alimony and child support made me flinch in panic. My ex-husband would visit occasionally leaving his usual $10 or $20 on top of the refrigerator, to which I just said thank you, wondering if he truly thought this money could take care of two children in the way they were accustomed. We were still officially married, and although I just wanted the saga to end, I was standing on the Biblical premise that "God hates divorce" and always made room for reconciliation. I never wanted to be outside His will; therefore, if divorce was the avenue our marriage would take my ex-husband would have to direct the traffic. T.D. Jakes, preaching at a marriage conference, stated that "separation and divorce causes bleeding", and in retrospect blood was being shed in our home, and would leave scars that only God could heal. Needless to say I needed a job and I needed it fast, so I prayed. God provided a job at a Christian company where I was a telemarketer for royal jelly products. Although it wasn't what I ever thought I would be doing, or what I wanted to do, it not only provided a weekly salary, but discounted vitamins for my family, and I was grateful. I worked with this company for about nine months while praying for direction. Though the days became easier, my finances were always too short to meet all the bills. However, I stepped out on nothing every day and watched God work miracles. I had come to know some attributes of God that I had never known and He became *"a very present help in time of trouble"*. (Psalm 46:1)

The apartment felt like it was caving in on us and became infested with worms like I had never seen. We came home everyday to these worms that I was deathly afraid of, however, my children constructed a way to kill them every day, and I actually depended on them to do it. Daily I would re-play Joel 2:25-26 in my mind; *"I will restore to you the years that the locusts has eaten, the cankerworm, and the caterpillar, and the palmerworm, my great army which I sent among you. You will have plenty to eat until you are full, and you will praise the name of the Lord your God".* God did not want us to live this way and would have to move us soon. Everything seemed like torture while living in this place, and I often wondered what the lesson I needed to learn here was, and I would hear God speak in the atmosphere "I am teaching you to trust me". A simple trip to the laundromat became an incredible exploit when it snowed, because we literally lived on a mountain. I would park the car at the bottom of the mountain and put the bags on my shoulder in an effort to get them into the house. If it snowed while on the way home from anywhere I would dread getting home, because I knew it would mean carrying my children and myself up that dreadful mountain. It sounds like we lived in the boonies, but it was still right there in Rockland County. Although we lived only minutes away from many of our church family, I can't remember ever having much company while living in that place so it became lonely and damp.

I realized quickly that if I was going to create a better life for us I would have to go back to school. I was 41 years old and the thought was repulsive to me. I started my Bachelors in 1979 and dropped out in 1983 with only one semester to go. I had acquired a good job at the time and thought I would never have to tread this path again. My dad had always said getting that degree would become vital to my future, but I never listened. I recall him repeating constantly, though he had no formal education, that "your education is something no one can take away from you". Now, at what I thought, the preposterous age of 41, I was about to launch myself into this overwhelming adventure while trying to raise two children. I braced myself, as I prepared to find the program that would work best for me. Since I started years ago as a Business major, I believed this was how I should finish. As I walked into the office of the advisor I had a lump in my throat; school was so different from what I remembered, as the technological age had taken over and I was the most computer illiterate person I knew. After I explained my situation she proceeded to explain a program that she referred to as "The Edge Program". I remember laughing as I affirmed to her that this was the program for me, recognizing I was currently living on the edge. She chuckled, even though she had no idea what I meant. I registered for school that day and was scheduled to begin the following February 2002.

Paul, in Ephesians 6:13 realized the believer's war was not one to be fought with arsenal like guns, because it's not against people, but spiritual armed forces in the invisible realm. Hence, these wicked forces will use people to do their dirty work. We are fighting satan and his cohorts, which include numerous spirits to be reckoned with. Therefore, I was not delusional, but stood my ground understanding that my spiritual life was at stake and the enemy would stop at nothing to take me out. Although I continued to attend church services, I have to admit it was torture at times. My ex-husband played at vital role at Bethel Gospel Assembly and I always thought I would stay in the background, never wanting to be in the front, but always happy about being a good helper in his ministry. I also derived great pleasure from teaching my Sunday school class, because I felt a genuine call to young people. However, when this saga was initiated I was asked by the Sunday school superintendent to step down from my role.

My heart was broken that night, as this had become my way of coping with all the losses I was facing. Hence, I made the decision to go to church and sit with my children in the balcony where I could not be seen or questioned. Church folks could be unknowingly insensitive at times, and since they didn't know exactly how to deal with the situation, it led to questions I was not equipped to answer. Some would stare in silence for fear of uttering the wrong thing. However, I choose to remember my church family at Bethel who rolled up their sleeves, stepped into the trenches and helped in ways that still baffle my mind.

I call to mind a special night right before Thanksgiving, as I wondered where I would get money for groceries. There was a knock on the door and I actually thought they were coming to repossess my car, however, when I opened the door there were bags of groceries everywhere. This and other acts of compassion happened a lot as God placed our family on the hearts of others in our church family, and they reciprocated by giving in any way they could. They were the essence of Proverbs 28:27, *"Those who give to the poor will lack nothing"*. I will never forget those extraordinary brothers and sisters in Christ who exercised incredible kindness during my storm, as they helped to keep me afloat, when at times I thought I would drown. I felt like the silver being made in the furnace, and although the heat at times was unbearable, knowing my church family was there always made everything easier to endure. God had placed me in this church and at every prospect of danger He reminded me that this storm was not about me but about all who would be helped through me. I must admit there were times when I wondered if God had forgotten about me, because I just couldn't see the handwriting on the wall, but I tried to remain still. The storm was still passing over and I was still standing, Hallelujah!!

I was still in search of a home suitable and affordable for my children and me. The desire was to continue living in Rockland County, and I searched tirelessly. This, however, was not what God had in mind and I needed to go with His flow and not my own. We eventually found a two bedroom apartment for us in a complex in Westchester County. While I wondered why God would move us so far away from all the support system and everything we knew, I recognize now that He wanted me to solely depend on

Him. It was a small apartment, but we had grown accustomed to the smaller things in life, therefore, it was seemingly huge to us. It was a sigh of relief coming off our Haverstraw mountain experience, so we never complained. I was still in financial difficulty and I thought at times this was a Job experience, and many times found myself studying the book of Job extensively, embracing his outcome as my own. Life had become a minute by minute experience, as I waited on God for complete healing in every facet. He, at times, seemed like He wasn't listening, but always showed up in the nick of time, proving Himself to be the omnipotent, omnipresent, and omniscient God that He is. Even though this was a slow process according to my time table, I knew that God's timing was always best and prayed earnestly for more patience. I was working in Kronos time but God was strategically planning in His Kairos timeframe, which I have to admit made me very anxious at times. My children would now change their school district for the fifth time and I knew it was a struggle. We were in this together and as I pressed I watched them do the same, most times without complaining.

My brother and his family lived close by so I was able to leave my children in their care when I needed to. They were a great help to me in so many ways, and when they broke the news that they would be moving to Florida I was crushed and so were my children. We had grown familiar to them being nearby and I wondered how things would be without them. Once again I believe God was in the midst teaching me how to be completely dependent on His care. My children found new friends and I became the neighborhood mom helping them with their lemonade stands and other events they were so quick to plan, at times, without my approval. Life was different in this town, but we stayed connected with our church family at Bethel, commuting fifty minutes back and forth to all events. Sometimes I would fall asleep at the wheel from all the driving, but God always kept us safe in our travels. 1Peter 1:6-7 says, *"In all this you greatly rejoice, though now for a little while you may have had to suffer grief in all kinds of trials. These have come so that the proven genuineness of your faith—of greater worth than gold, which perishes even though refined by fire—may result in praise, glory and honor when Jesus Christ is revealed."* I was being kept by the power of God and I knew it every day. The tests that I had to endure were creating a powerful testimony for others who would have to gain healing as a result. My faith was being proven and although enduring was tough at times, the Lover of my soul was revealing to me that He was continuously sufficient.

On December 22nd 2002 one day before what would have been my 13th wedding anniversary, I received final divorce papers. In retrospect, even though I saw it coming, it still felt like I was being kicked in the gut and unable to breathe. The two years of separation saga that had begun in 2000 had reached its final plateau ending in divorce and not reconciliation, like I had hoped. I knew God hated divorce and wondered what this would mean for my future. What would this mean as it pertained to ministry? What did the future hold for me? Would the loneliness ever go away? Would it be okay to one day re-marry? How would I deplete myself of the sexual urges that still lingered within? The questions mounted as I stood in my kitchen looking at this piece of paper that marked the end of an era in my life. There was a knot in my stomach that could only be relieved when I stood over the commode and regurgitated. It seemed like a very bad dream, but it was very real, and it was necessary to throw up the old to make room for the new. I tried to hold back the tears, but they flowed freely. Time stood still for me that day and I asked the Lord to put His arms around me and bring comfort. I sat in silence for the rest of the day and to bring comfort that night God gave me *"weeping may endure for a night, but joy cometh in the morning."* (Psalm 30:5) I looked forward with great anticipation for the morning of joy that would gradually come, as I put my life in the Hands of the One who knew me best; my Everlasting Father, Abba, King of kings.

1Corinthians 13 4-8 had become the signature verse for me and my children as I read it to them every single night after their dad made his exit. It was a night like any other as I proceeded to read, but they had fallen asleep and I was actually reading out loud to myself. I got to verse 5 which states *"love does not dishonor others, it is not self-seeking, it is not easily angered, **and it keeps no record of wrongs."*** It was as if God literally entered the room and the words **"it keeps no record of wrongs"** kept ringing in my ear as I knew I needed to forgive this man, and the woman who used the ungodly weapons at her disposal to lure him away from God and family. How was I going to do this incredibly hard thing? I knew only God could help, so I closed my eyes and simply asked Him to help. This would prove to be yet another hard thing I would have to do, but I knew this would be the foundation for complete healing and wholeness. About one week later after praying incessantly about this, I picked up the phone and proceeded to dial his number. My hands shook as I thought about what I would say. He answered in that all too familiar soft tone that had won my heart on that unforgettable singles retreat that led to our marriage. I remember, as if it was yesterday, declaring I would forgive him for all he had done. I felt release almost immediately and although this would be a process, it was the beginning of all the new things that God had in store for me as I went forward on this journey of life.

Life as I knew it had ended and with God's help I was still standing against all the attacks of the enemy. Although I fell to the floor a few times, I would never stay there long enough to accept defeat. No matter how many times I got struck I was determined to be a winner in this war, so I put my boxing gloves on and got back in the ring. I had a barrage of people watching me from the sidelines and I had to prove to the ones who didn't know my Jesus that He was their ultimate source; and to those wavering in their faith that turning back to the world was not the way to go. I felt like Paul when he declared, *"I know what it is to be in need, and I know what it is to have plenty. I have learned the secret of being content in any and every situation, whether well fed or hungry, whether living in plenty or in want"*. (Philippians 4:12) I was living in want at the moment, but I could hear the Lord whispering "this day won't last forever". My mother, who had remained permanently in Jamaica after my dad's passing, would come to visit each summer to help with the children. I looked forward with great anticipation to her summer visits and it put a glimmer of hope on my children's faces each time we went to get her at the airport. They loved their grandma Lena, who they lovingly referred to as "gramma Nina".

I registered for a discipleship course being offered at Bethel. We met every Sunday morning and I learned so much about myself. At times it took me away from self and allowed me the opportunity to focus on and pray for others in the group. I looked forward to those Sunday mornings when I would meet and share with these awesome people of God. It was during these sessions that God gave me the rhema word in Jeremiah 1:7-10 *"You must go to everyone I send you to and say whatever I command you. Do not be afraid of them, for I am with you and will rescue you," declares the LORD. Then the LORD reached out his hand and touched my mouth and said to me, "Now, I have put my words in your mouth. See, today I appoint you over nations and kingdoms to uproot and tear down, to destroy and overthrow, to build and to plant."*Although I didn't quite comprehend what God was telling me at the time, it was clear that all the turmoil was not about me, but how He would use me in the life of others; and bring me to a place requiring me to bind the hands of the enemy setting captives free in Jesus name. This was a miracle in the making and I could either ignore or go full force into the fiery furnace, proving to the masses that my God would not allow me to burn. I chose to go with the latter and became unstoppable in the process. Family and friends watched as a complete metamorphosis took place as I became determined to walk into my destiny without looking back. God had positioned me to do great exploits and although I had found myself in a warzone I knew I was equipped to fight and win.

Chapter 4

Still Standing

"So, stand with the belt of truth round you. And wear the breastplate of righteousness". Ephesians 6:14

This belt of truth that Paul speaks of being girded with in Ephesians 6:14 is the truth of the gospel. As believers in this fight we need to be yielded and totally surrendered to the God of truth. This belt that I hung on to for sustenance was the ultimate tool that would keep me standing in the midst of my perfect storm. It was perfect because I was not in it alone, but my Savior was steering the ship and He knew how much I could bear. I had to believe He would never leave nor forsake me, and when I felt like falling down He would carry me. What a mighty God He is, who keeps every promise to heal, restore, and make whole. In Psalm 46:1-2 the psalmist affirms, *"God is our refuge and strength, an ever present help in trouble. Therefore, we will not fear, though the earth gives way and the mountains fall into the heart of the sea, though its waters roar and foam and the mountains quake with their surging".* In verse 10 he says *"Be still, and know that I am God; I will be exalted among the nations, I will be exalted in the earth."* These scriptures gripped my soul every time I read them throughout this journey, and continue to do so even as I pen these pages. God had kept His promises and was truly an ever present help in my troubles. He had been, and remains healer, forgiver, and friend.

The question of whether I would function in ministry again was quickly answered, as I was asked to re-join the Sunday school ministry, teaching older teens and young adults. As I entered the room for the first time in what seemed like an eternity, I would meet the same students I taught prior to being asked to relinquish my post. It was an honor and a privilege to be teaching and investing time in their lives again. I was armed and ready to stand uncovered before them, in an effort to help them live holy before God. Those students became part of the anchor that would continue to keep me afloat in my perfect storm. As I have had the privilege to watch some of them grow into spiritually infectious adults, it makes my heart glad.

Alabaster Women of Faith, the women's ministry at Bethel also played an instrumental role in my being able to pray for and help bring healing to many women. When asked to be on the board of directors for that ministry I was privileged and thrilled that God would use me in this way. In 2005 I was asked to be the assistant director of the ministry, and thought to myself how humorous God was, in allowing me to use everything that the enemy meant for my demise to bring new life to those I would touch. I also taught in the Bible school of this awesome church and came to recognize that although I had always been comfortable in my behind the scenes role that I played while married; there was a strategic role in ministry that God wanted me to play and He had used every event in my life to prepare me. I was ready to take the reins and run with whatever God was about to do.

In fall 2002, as stated earlier, I started my academic journey at Mercy College. I remember thinking that was the perfect name for the school, because they most definitely showed mercy to me. I proceeded to complete my Bachelors that I started in 1979 utilizing the Edge Program; majoring in Organizational Management. The program was rigorous as one was expected to finish a normal sixteen week semester in eight weeks. I would enter each class with a resolve to complete it with a perfect grade. School would become the place where I would ultimately find my voice and become what I believed God had destined me to be. I had a plan to become a teacher and therefore, knew this was only the beginning, as I would venture to do a Master's in education. I had always been drawn to young people and wanted to give back to that generation in an effort to help re-direct their thoughts towards learning. My hope was to hinder as many as I could from throwing in the towel and dropping out of school like I did. I was starting my life all over and I have to admit at times it was petrifying. The world of school had changed tremendously since I last attended, and the technological venue was in full blast. I was a technological buffoon and the computer was my enemy. However, this was the era I was now living in and I could either embrace it or shun it. I chose to do the former and did it at times with great hesitation and fear. I registered for a computer class as part of my course work so I could befriend this man made machine, that would be instrumental in everything that I would achieve. This had become an adventure for me as I pressed toward the mark determined to win in every arena. During this school adventure I took a psychology class that I found extremely interesting. I recall the professor, a short Jewish man with a long beard, stating he never gave A's, and I was unwavering in proving him wrong. I received an A in that course and so many others and since he was the chairperson for the department, he went on to recommend me for the psychology program after only one course. I finished that Edge Program in record time, and in 2003 I walked across the stage to accept my diploma graduating Suma Cum Laude. What an honor, as I listened to my children cheering me on from the audience.

I recognized at this stage in the game that if I wanted to work with the youth of society I needed to pursue a new career in the school system. Once again I looked to the one I call Father and realized that I would have to start at the bottom and work my way up. Could my family survive another financial crisis? We were just beginning to gain momentum, but I had to make this tough decision. As I walked up the driveway to my friend's house one afternoon, still contemplating what to do and how to get my foot in the door of the public school system, I literally fell off my high heel shoes. It was very painful, but vanity persuaded me to put those shoes back on and keep moving. I was feeling pain, but it was not unbearable so I drove home and completed my usual errands like any other day. When I woke up the next morning my ankle was swollen and very stiff, and I could hardly place my foot on the ground. I drove myself to the emergency room only to find out I had broken my ankle and had to stay off my feet for at least six weeks, which meant no driving and no work. While lying in bed one afternoon feeling sorry for myself, I decided to look through the yellow pages for a school that would hire me. There were so many schools in Westchester County to choose from, and I literally remember closing my eyes and asking God to allow my fingers to open to the right one. I called a school that day that I had never heard of and the voice on the phone said they were looking for a one on one teacher assistant for an autistic student, and wanted me to come for an interview immediately. I drove on a broken ankle that day and limped into the interview on crutches. As soon as I returned home there was a phone call and the voice on the other end said congratulations you got the job. I had mixed emotions as I had no idea what it entailed to work with autistic children, and the pay was unbelievably low. I remember telling a friend what my salary would be and she replied, "I didn't know people still

worked for that type of salary", however, I wasn't just
people I was a soldier in service for the Lord. I was once
again called upon to exercise mammoth faith and I just
looked up and asked God to help me.

The job started that September and although I had done
a lot of research about autism, it did not prepare me for the
second grade student I was about to meet. She had been
diagnosed as Asperger (a developmental disorder related to
autism and characterized by higher than average
intellectual ability coupled with impaired social skills and
restrictive, repetitive patterns of interest and activities), and
had almost no social skills. She would be my introduction
to a disability that I have since learned so much about. She
stepped on my foot every day and trampled the other
children like a truck gone wild. This was going to be the
job that would either make or break me as I recognized
immediately it would be a challenge. I worked hard with
this little girl and at every stage I added a new tool to my
scholastic tool belt. I had always been reluctant to be in the
presence of people with disabilities, and now I was the
instrument that would hopefully be used to at least steer
this little person to develop social skills that would propel

her through school. I prayed each day for wisdom, as I became intrigued with this child and her constant companion, autism. At the conclusion of that year I was asked to work in the Middle school as a teacher assistant for not just one, but several students with disabilities most of whom had some form of autism. I would work for four years with these children and in the summers work with a student who would literally lick my arm each morning as he exited the school bus, thinking because I was black it would taste like chocolate. I often wondered when he would get the message that it didn't, but he never did. The job was tedious and the pay check was low, but this was to be used as a stepping stone to my future so I persevered.

I continued my education at Mercy College in 2003 with thoughts of becoming a school psychologist. This was fascinating, but I constantly felt the need to switch gears and delve into something more rewarding. I registered for a counseling practicum course and this is where I found my niche. With twenty one credits of psychology towards my Masters, I switched allegiance to pursue a degree in counseling. Each class gave me the impetus to keep moving forward, and the Jeremiah 29:11 words I received some years prior were beginning to flesh out in my life. God truly did have a plan to prosper, and although not always financially, if I held on to His hand I would be guided every step of the way. Psalm 73:28 says *"As for me, it is good to be near God. I have made the Sovereign Lord my refuge; I will tell of all your deeds"*. If I stayed near to God He would be my safe haven and one day I would be given the platform to tell of all His deeds. I continued in my passion for my exceptional students while studying incessantly to get to my goal. The classes were more difficult, but I had a secret weapon called prayer. My 2am morning study ritual became a lifestyle, and at times I would even have to take my children to school with me, but I was determined to accomplish this feat and nothing or no one would hinder me.

Though not the norm, as a result of my tenure in the school where I was appointed a teacher assistant, I was given the opportunity to complete a large portion of my internship while still working full time for pay. God had granted me favour with my colleagues and I was grateful. I recall my first client during my internship being a thirteen year old African American female. This was unusual, as the students in this school district were predominantly Caucasian. When she walked into the room I immediately knew this was not going to be an ordinary session. I came from behind the desk and positioned myself next to her on the couch. She proceeded to explain her plans to take her life that night, and although I remained outwardly calm, I almost fell off the seat. I managed to perform all the tasks necessary for that session with a calm demeanour. The professionals who sat with me in the room were awe struck at the way I handled the situation, but I knew in my heart that God was with me, and would always be the true counselor in the room on every occasion. The time came for me to take my comprehensive exam and I passed with flying colors, and when asked what the topic for my thesis would be I didn't hesitate as I knew it would be "autism". I walked across that familiar stage in May 2006 to receive what I thought was my final degree, a Master of Science degree in counseling. To God be the glory great things He had done and would continue to do. It felt like the conclusion to yet another era in my life, but I knew in my heart it was only the beginning of a new adventure. I was poised and ready, and I joined my brother Paul in

Philippians 3:13 in saying, *"Not that I have already obtained all this, or have already been made perfect, but I press on to take hold of that for which Christ Jesus took hold of me."*

It was an unbelievable feeling as I had not only received a Master's degree but had also acquired twenty one credits in psychology along the way. I felt like I could conquer the world and nothing could possibly stand in my way. Life quickly set in as I realized I now had to seek a new job and I put my feelers out, believing God would provide a lucrative job for me as a school counselor. It was more difficult than I thought it would be, but nothing in comparison to what I had already faced on this journey, so I patiently waited on God. While surfing the net in my search I bumped into Master's International School of Divinity. The school offered a Doctoral degree in Biblical counselling/Biblical studies, something I never even thought I would do, however, and on a whim, with no money to speak of I applied.

I once again hit a bump in the road and I had to sacrifice my phone for a season as I was unable to pay the telephone bill. We went without a phone for about a month as I continued my search for a job. The phone was finally restored and we had grown so accustomed to not having one when it rang we were startled by the sound. When I picked up the receiver it was the unfamiliar voice of the president of Master's International School of Divinity inquiring if I was still interested in attending their school. I had completely forgotten about applying and explained that although I was interested, I was in dire straits financially and would have to pursue that degree at another time. He immediately began to pray for God to kindle a fire under my ministry and grant me the opportunity to attend the school and complete that doctorate. I gave him my cell phone number, and recall laughing when I hung up the phone, because I thought to myself how humorous God was. The school year ended and I resigned my teaching assistant job believing God was about to open a new door.

I had not seen my brother and his family since they moved to Florida four years earlier so I looked for an affordable flight deciding to take my children on a well-deserved vacation. We were excited as we had not been anywhere in so long, and looked forward to visiting with family. We got off the plane in West Palm Beach, Florida in June 2006 for a two week vacation. My then sister in law graciously accommodated us and chauffeured us wherever we wanted to go. This was a great trip because it would afford me the opportunity to see my sister Joy and her family, and my best friend Sharon and her children, who also lived in Florida and I had not seen them in years. What a reunion it was, but I still wondered what I would do as it pertained to work when I returned home. This was a great vacation, but I had no job to return to and very little money in the bank, yet I refused to worry. I was here to have some long awaited fun with my children, and would do just that. My sister in law suggested that I search the internet for a job in the St. Lucie County school district where they lived, but I had no intention of moving to Florida, so I continued searching the New York schools. I received no responses and became concerned. I prayed and believed God to do something miraculous, but there was no New York job in sight. I was in a race and every time I thought I came to the finish line thinking I was winning, the finish line moved, and I had to position myself to move to the next level in God.

I made the decision to apply to the St. Lucie County School Board. I received a reply the next day from a high school in the area asking me to come for an interview the very next day. I was totally unprepared, but I collected my thoughts and dressed as appropriately as I could and walked into that office seemingly ready for anything and everything. As the questions came across the table I realized how God had equipped me over the years for this moment. During the interview I was asked if I would be pursuing a doctorate and I emphatically replied yes, not knowing how or when I would ever be able to meet the expense of school again. That too was a dream, but God had supernaturally fulfilled so many other dreams, it would be amiss to think this was too difficult for Him. The interview was successful and I was told the job was ninety nine percent mine, and I should pack my things and prepare to make the biggest move of my life. As I drove back to my brother's house I wondered what this would mean for my children, and if God truly wanted me to relinquish everything familiar and move to a new state. This was a major decision and I had to think, not only of myself, but what this would mean as it pertained to the distance between my children and their father. When I told them about the job offer they were excited about the move, especially my son who had experienced some unnerving times in school and wanted desperately to try something new. When I called to break the news to their dad it was as if he already knew what I was about to say. I could hear the sobbing through the phone as he begged me not to move away with his children. This was a hard decision and I needed definite confirmation from God.

With the help of my sister in law I found a brand new three bedroom two bathroom house, renting for less than I was paying in N.Y. for my small two bedroom apartment. It seemed like everything was falling into place, but I still wanted clarification from the One I call Father. We travelled back to N.Y. by plane and I spent the entire plane ride trying to figure out how I would pack all my things, break my lease, find a truck and driver, and take that long drive back to Florida. This was BIG and my brain was thinking at a pace much faster than it had ever thought before. As I began to tell all my friends and church family what I was about to do, I could hear the shock in some of their voices, but no one tried to hinder me from going not even my Bishop. I collected boxes and began packing, but there was still urgency in my spirit to get my marching orders from God. This was a place in my life that I had never visited before and my sole desire was to be in God's will.

On July 18, 2006, one week prior to leaving, while sitting on the bed in the morning to have my devotions, the Lord gave me *"Now what I am commanding you today is not too difficult for you or beyond your reach. It is not up in heaven, so that you have to ask, "Who will ascend into heaven to get it and proclaim it to us so we may obey it?"Nor is it beyond the sea, so that you have to ask, "Who will cross the sea to get it and proclaim it to us so we may obey it?"No, the word is very near you; it is in your mouth and in your heart so you may obey it.See, I set before you today life and prosperity, death and destruction. For I command you today to love the LORD your God, to walk in obedience to him, and to keep his commands, decrees and laws; then you will live and increase, and the LORD your God will bless you in the land you are entering to possess. This day I call the heavens and the earth as witnesses against you that I have set before you life and death, blessings and curses. Now choose life, so that you and your children may live and that you may love the LORD your God, listen to his voice, and hold fast to him.* "Deuteronomy 30:11-16 and 19-20 God impressed on my heart that He was taking me to this city for a specific reason and if I just remained obedient I would be blessed. I knew immediately that the Holy Spirit was tugging at my heart to be obedient and move into this new, still somewhat underdeveloped city, to inflict mayhem and infuse spiritual revival. Tears welled up in my eyes as I thought about what I was being asked to do. I was given my marching orders that day and although it felt like I was leaving everything near and dear to me in New York, I had to embrace my new surroundings and wait for God to strategically use me. He had already told me years prior that *"You must go to everyone I send you to and say whatever I command you. Do not be afraid of them, for I am with you and will rescue you."* (Jeremiah 1:7-8) Therefore, although I thought I was relocating to find a job that I had worked very hard academically to acquire, God had other plans that he would reveal to me one bit at a time.

Chapter 5

New Beginnings

"And with your feet fitted with the readiness that comes from the gospel of peace".
Ephesians 6:15

My friend and confidant Rosie, although I think had mixed emotions, showed up to help like she has always done since we lived in her home, in what seemed like a lifetime prior, and continues to do to this day. She helped me pack for what was to be the most courageous trip of my life. I must concede that I was very nervous, not only about where I was going, but the long drive that awaited me and my children. I knew they also had emotions that they were not expressing as they clung to my every move trusting me to take care of them. In Ephesians 6:15 Paul continues his dialogue about the armor, encouraging the believer to put on the gospel of peace like shoes. In essence this must be well fitted shoes, ready to be used on any occasion. I received this word as an exhortation to be ready to present the gospel of Jesus Christ in any venue that I would face in this town that I was about to call home. I needed a truck, but money was sparse, as it always seemed to be. God once again granted me favor as the church family at Bethel again came to the rescue. Bishop Brown found some men with willing hearts to drive the moving truck the night before we left, so all the necessities would be in place when we arrived at our destination. This was brotherly love in action and I will never forget the sacrifice of time and energy that was made on my family's behalf.

I sat in the car on July 25, 2006, making sure my children were secure in the back seat, as we ventured out on what would be the road trip of our lives. I prayed that God would cover us and take us to our destination safely. We headed to Georgia first to visit my friend Beverley and her family. This was done in an effort to rest before proceeding on to our destination in Florida. It would be about a ten hour trip and I was exhausted, and my legs were numb. When we arrived her husband looked at us and shook his head in unbelief that we were even there, and refused to allow us to leave in the morning like we planned. He beckoned us to stay as long as we needed so I could re-group. I was glad for the offer as my body felt like someone had hung me out to dry, as I had never driven that long before. As previously stated, I had literally taught myself to drive again some years earlier, after that almost fateful car accident, so this was an adventure that words cannot explain. We stayed for a day and I got back in the car and continued on what I choose to call "a journey to remember". It would take an additional fifteen hours to finally get to our destination. Every time I thought about ministry and all that I had left in my New York comfort zone, I felt the tears well up in my eyes. However, God had given me His approval and had gone ahead of me to prepare the way. I thought a lot about the Biblical characters and missionaries who had received similar directives from God and how they must have felt. It seemed like an endless drive, but my children continued to be troopers, especially my son as he stayed awake talking and feeding me sour patch candy to keep me awake and alert. We arrived at my brother's home in the afternoon of July 27, 2006 tired and weary, but elated about the new beginnings that were about to unfold.

I was scheduled to begin working in the high school in a week and I got busy that Monday morning registering my children for yet another new school. My son was seemingly elated at the thought of going to a new school, as his school experiences to date had been fear-provoking as he continuously faced bullying attacks from his peers. My daughter, however, had mixed emotions as she had already completed her first year in high school and would miss the friends and companions she had acquired. At times I felt she really didn't want this move, but just settled for a change in location because she felt it would be best for our family. As I proceeded to register them I could at times see the tears trying to come from Shanae's eyes, and I knew she was missing her familiar surroundings of school and church in New York. I now comprehend how Abraham must have felt when God asked him to leave the familiar and venture into the unknown. *"The LORD had said to Abram, "Go from your country, your people and your father's household to the land I will show you".*(Genesis12:1) This was a challenge and my children were caught in the shuffle. Although they didn't say much their eyes spoke volumes, and I think at times they wondered if their mother had lost her mind, in asking them to relinquish their city mentality and move to such a seemingly uninteresting town. However, since we did not yet move into our permanent address we used my brother's and they were both registered for school.

I drove them to school on that first morning and my son kissed me good bye with a smile on his face. I remember him saying "don't worry mommy I will be fine". I am not sure if he meant it, but it brought a comforting feeling to my heart as I drove away and watched him in the rear view mirror. As I continued to my daughter's school I heard a whimpering in the back seat. As I glanced across my shoulder I saw the tears that she had managed to suppress to this point, running down her face. She tried to explain the grief and discomfort she felt about moving and although her words were muffled by the tears, I knew exactly what she was trying to convey. I wondered, and even inquired, why she had waited until this point to express her feelings, pretending she was happy when all the time she was extremely sad. I searched for a school counselor who could help familiarize her with the school and probably pair her with someone who she could befriend. This continued for many weeks of school, until she finally grew accustomed to her environment.

I waited by the phone to hear when I would begin my new job as I had not been given an official date, but there was no phone call for days. I finally picked up the phone and listened as the familiar voice of the person who interviewed me told me the job had been given to someone else. I was crushed. How was I supposed to take care of my family without an income? What exactly was God doing? Did I hear Him correctly or had I convinced myself that this was His will? I sat on the couch in the living room of my new rented house having no idea how I was going to keep living there. This was a dilemma and it would be fine if I were alone, but I had two young people always depending on me to do the correct thing, and I felt like I had let them down. The doorbell rang and in walked my sister in law. She asked if I was just going to sit on the couch waiting for something to happen, to which I had no reply. I think I was in shock at the thought that I had uprooted my family from everything they knew and loved, and drove twenty five hours to hear someone say I did not get the job. How would I explain this to my children? And what should I do next? I believe my sister in law saw the perplexed look on my face and she prayed like I have never heard her pray before. She had a newspaper in her hand and had circled a job that she thought would be a good choice based on my schooling. I called the number listed and was given an interview one day later.

The job was in Martin County about 30 minutes away, and though I had no idea where I was going, I got in my car the next day, with the directions that had been given to me on the phone. The interview was short, but I learned right away that I would be a mental health counselor traveling throughout the schools in that county to meet with students with behavior and mental health difficulties. I also learned that at times I would be asked to conduct home visits for those students who did not report to school for a length of time. I never dreamed that my career as a counselor would begin this way, but I recognized that God had prepared me with my first middle school suicidal client that I had encountered during my internship. The salary was less than the school counselor job I was previously offered, but it was a larger salary than I had ever seen. Although I felt unequipped for this fork in the road, once again I had to depend on God to guide me, as I walked on deep water to get to the other side. Scripture declares *"And when the disciples saw him walking on the sea, they were troubled, saying, it is a spirit; and they cried out for fear. But straightway Jesus spake unto them saying, Be of good cheer, it is I; be not afraid".* (Matthew 14:26-27) I related to the disciples here. Jesus knew they were frightened just as He knew I was frightened, and He quickly calmed their fear by speaking, just as He calmed my fear with His Spirit that day, as my voice quivered in acceptance of the position. In verse 28 Peter spoke *"Lord, if it be thou, bid me come unto thee on the water"*. Like Peter, I still had some doubts as to whether God had truly called me to this place, but I had been saved for a long time just like Peter, and needed to know without a shadow of a doubt that I had heard my Master's voice and there was no turning back.

I ventured out to my new job the following Monday, with butterflies in my stomach and Jesus on my mind. As I listened to the directives from my new supervisor I knew this would not be easy, but nothing I had done in the past six years was, so I took a deep breath. As I walked into the first school and sat at the desk that was provided, a thirteen year old African American male walked in the room with the worse look of anger on his face. He walked towards me balled up his fist and proceeded to punch a hole in the wall right above my head. Though I shook in my boots I heard myself calmly say "did that hurt"? With blood coming from his still balled up fist he answered "yes ma'am". I recall saying softly "so you will not be doing that again, right? He replied once again "no ma'am". This marked the beginning of my new job, and my new life in Florida. I went daily from school to school, not only meeting new students but new adults, becoming familiar with the school counselors and staff in each one. Everyone commended me on how well I was performing my task, and even though it was not the job I would have chosen, I knew God had a plan and a reason and would reveal it slowly as He had always done with me.

I interacted a lot with school counselors as I familiarized myself with the public school system hoping to one day still be employed with St. Lucie County schools. In dialoguing with one of the male counselors I was asked if I had ever considered being an adjunct professor to gain additional income. Since I had only just received my Master's degree, I thought it highly improbable that I would be considered for such a position. However, he gave me a number to call Palm Beach Atlantic University, a Christian based college in West Palm Beach. I had never heard of this school, and all I remembered about Palm Beach was the airport where we landed for our vacation in June. However, if given the opportunity for an interview I would not pass up the chance. I called the number he gave me, inquiring about an adjunct teaching position, but never thinking I would be given the occasion to go any further. I sent all the credentials I was asked for via email and was asked to come for an interview. As I drove on the highway to my forty five minute destination, I wondered what God was cooking up for me this time? My unfamiliarity with the area got me extremely lost, but I soon found my way to my destination, fifteen minutes late and sweating profusely. I walked into a room of about five people with the label doctor attached to their names, but surprisingly I was neither nervous nor uncomfortable. I felt like a perfect fit in the room. They proceeded to ask me questions one at a time, but I remained calm as I answered each one. I recall one question being "how would you incorporate your faith into your teaching"? I knew that was orchestrated just for me. I answered unequivocally how I would do that, recognizing immediately that my answer pleased the people in the room. I was offered the adjunct position immediately, with my first class to begin in January 2007. As I sat in my car about to drive home, I remember laughing hysterically and pinching myself. I knew this had very little to do with my credentials, but God had shown up and granted me favor with this interviewing committee. This move of God would eventually allow me the opportunity to teach as an adjunct professor in other venues, giving me the platform to teach counseling skills to so many.

I continued working as a mental health counselor and was relentless in my pursuit to be the best I could be. At times when asked to conduct home visits I would drive up to places that looked like no one could possibly live there. I can remember sitting in my car at times in front of these homes just praying for safety. Sometimes, as I crossed the threshold of these dwellings I would be met by an abundance of creepy crawly things, and the scent in the homes would be atrocious. It made me realize how blessed I was, and no matter how difficult life had been God had truly blessed me in so many ways. After two months of working in this area of counseling I had learned a lot, not just about my young clients, but about myself. Philippians 1:6 explains, *"Being confident of this, that he who began a good work in you will carry it on to completion until the day of Christ Jesus."* God had started a great work in me and this job was a bridge to completing it. Though at first this work seemed tedious and frustrating and the pay was less than I expected, I knew it was the stimulus that would drive me to the next step of this awesome journey.

One October afternoon in 2006, while grocery shopping in Walmart, two months after I started the position my cell phone rang. As I answered the phone a pleasant female voice on the other end asked if I was still interested in working for St. Lucie County schools as a school counselor. I immediately said yes, and she proceeded to explain that it was a leave replacement position in an elementary school, and not middle school or high school as I had hoped. The counselor had left for a year and would be returning the following school year in June 2007. Although my desire was to work in the school system, I had to be realistic in my thoughts as I would be giving up a permanent job for a temporary one. I also remembered I had signed a contract during my interview for the current job, stipulating I would work for a year. In essence, I was still on probation, as I had not yet even worked ninety days. However, I went on the interview. As I walked into the room I realized right away that the female African American principal sitting behind the desk was a kindred spirit, and there was an immediate connection. She hired me that day, but I still felt an allegiance to my current job, and always desired that my integrity be left intact. I wrote, what I think, was the most incredible resignation letter I would ever write, never wanting to burn any bridges behind me. I had grown accustomed to my surroundings and though I was only on the job a short time, I would miss it all. My letter was accepted with a glowing response, and I started my new position two weeks later.

There I was in the middle of a somewhat large office as counselor to over 500 students grades K-5, who would look to me for guidance and counsel. As I sat in the chair for the first time, not knowing exactly what was expected of me, I reflected on the second grade special education student, who had started me some five years ago on this road to a counseling career. I wondered what had become of her and all the others, and if anything I said or did had made a difference. Though I had been given the opportunity to intern in a school, nothing prepared me for St. Lucie County Schools. I immediately knew that if I was going to succeed in this system I would need to relinquish my New York hat and start blooming where I was planted. One of my first encounters was with a nine year old Caucasian girl who was referred to me by teachers because she was urinating in her pants every day. On our third encounter as I spoke to her using as much play therapy as possible, she told of her mother's tragic death in the home. She talked about missing her and currently having to live with her dad and brother in the house. She ventured to explain how her dad would enter her room every night, get on top of her and go up and down. Immediately the atmosphere in the room changed as I had to take action to protect this little girl and make sure she was safe. Her dad was arrested that afternoon when he came to pick her up from school, and I would be subpoenaed to court some time later. This laid the foundation for what would be a very challenging profession.

The year was coming to a close and I still had no idea if or where I would be placed for the upcoming school year. However, on the home front my niece was about to be married and I had planned a bridal shower to be held in my home. The night prior to the event I had the most vivid dream of my mom dying and me attending her funeral. She had been living in Jamaica since the death of my dad in 1995. When I called Jamaica I was told that my mom was perfectly fine and I was able to speak with her for a short while. The next morning the phone rang and it was my adopted sister Velma, who lived with and took care of my parents in their senior years. Her voice screeched as she managed to tell me that my mom had fallen while trying to exit the bed and was now limping. While it seemed like she would be fine I received yet another phone call, explaining that she was unable to walk and the doctor's pronounced that her hip was broken and they would have to do surgery. Each time they were about to perform the surgery my mother developed another complication and the surgery was postponed. I decided I needed to pay a visit to my mom, and did so with my brother. I stayed for a week and spent some quality time with her. She constantly spoke of her grandchildren and how she would miss us when she was gone. I believe she knew she was on her last leg of this life, and one week after returning to Florida, on a Good Friday morning in 2007, my sister in law showed up at the front door, pronouncing the devastating news that my mother had passed away. I remember thinking she was finally with her beloved Ira after twelve years of waiting.

Prior to going to Jamaica I was told by my principal that she mentioned me to another principal at a meeting. They were building a Middle school addition to an elementary school and were seeking a school counselor. She gave rave reviews about me and after a ten minute interview I was offered the position. The job was scheduled to begin in May, after returning from my mother's funeral. It was a very emotional time and I had not really grieved my mom, however, I was ready for a permanent job and this would be it. As I drove to get to my new job that first morning, I remember having to pull to the side of the road. My eyes were flooded with tears as I cried uncontrollably. I had not cried like that in years and I believe it was a moment of healing for me. As I sat in the parked car by myself I remember thinking how much life had changed for me, and that this was yet the end of another period. In John 14:27 Jesus declares *"Peace I leave with you; my peace I give you. I do not give to you as the world gives. Do not let your hearts be troubled and do not be afraid."* Both my parents were now deceased and my heavenly Father gave me an overpowering sense of peace. What a mighty God we serve when in moments like these we can dissolve into His arms and refuel for the journey.

I was entering a new season and I had to position myself strategically, even when working in the secular arena. This was a brand new Middle school in a new building, and as I sat in the new chair behind my new desk, everything around me was new even the scent in the atmosphere. I had gone from the seat in the corner of a second grade classroom, with an autistic little girl who stepped on my foot every day, to a brand new Middle school in a completely new state ready to accomplish new exploits. The scripture I was given prior to leaving New York rushed to the forefront of my mind, as I remembered God promising blessing, and all I had to do was obey Him. I enjoyed those foundational years at the school and managed to use my creativity to implement some new things. I realized quickly that I was not just the counselor, but had a myriad of other tasks to perform, always managing to perform each one with tenacity and flare. This was all God's doing and I knew it. He had embellished me with gifts and talents along the way and was now allowing me to flourish. Isaiah 43:19 says *"See, I am doing a new thing! Now it springs up; do you not perceive it? I am making a way in the wilderness and streams in the wasteland"*. God was about to do a new thing and I seized the moment to walk into my destiny. Although I was hired as the Middle School counselor there was so much more to this complex job. New York was my training ground and now I was expected to flesh out what I had learned, and include things I had never been taught. I knew I was under a microscope and there were even those who expected me to fail, but I am a child of the King. It was very difficult to start a new school, but I have proven, with God's help over the past seven years, that I can truly *"do all things through Christ who gives me strength"*.

Although things seemed to be falling into place with my career, I was still in exploration of a church that my family could call home. We had spent some months attending my brother's church, but something seemed to be missing. Ministry had become my life over the years and I knew from all the directives I had received from the Master, this would just be an extension of what was started in New York. The scripture that declares, *"Being confident of this, that he who began a good work in you will carry it on to completion until the day of Christ Jesus"* was becoming a reality, and God was birthing ministry. However, I desired a church that would allow me to give birth to what God had conceived. There were many churches in this town, but we quickly realized that none was comparable with our beloved Bethel. I was so disappointed, but I prayed for God to lead us to a place where we could establish a new church family. I took off my Bethel hat and believed God to lead us to the right place. For months we visited churches and at times had church in our living room. In December 2007 my daughter attended a birthday celebration where she learned about a church called New Testament Faith Center. We visited the next Sunday and when we walked in the dance ministry was dancing through the aisles. As a result of my daughter's love for dance, she seemed to recognize immediately that this was the place for us. With questions still flooding my mind I conceded to give this a try and we began to attend regularly.

In 2008 after attending this church for a few months I made the decision to become a member of the ministry. Though this was not exactly what I was used to, it became church for me and my family as I attended regularly. The people became my new church family, although I continued to make reference to my church family in New York. I realized early that if I was going to make my mark in this town I needed a new attitude, even as it pertained to the politics of church. In February 2008 after attending a few youth services I was asked to be the Youth Pastor. When I left New York I remember declaring that youth ministry was behind me and something I wouldn't attach myself to again. This decision was made as a result of the many years working with young people in church and with New Horizons Ministry in New York, and realizing that I was burnt out from the experience. However, when asked by the pastor to pray about it God immediately gave me Romans 8:30 *"And those he predestined, he also called; those he called, he also justified; those he justified, he also glorified"*; 1 Corinthians 1:9 *"God is faithful, who has called you into fellowship with his Son, Jesus Christ our Lord"*; Ephesians 4:1 *"As a prisoner for the Lord, then, I urge you to live a life worthy of the calling you have received"*. God was obviously reminding me that this wasn't about my agenda but His, therefore, irrespective of how I felt He was calling me to do this for what I thought would be a short season. Consequently, I worked in this ministry for two and a half years before God released me. It was an intense season, as I sought the Lord daily for help. Working in that ministry allowed me the opportunity to gain knowledge of the community, as I invested time in planning and preparing for each event. I would move forward to accomplish so many other things in this church, and eventually also be a part of the leadership team for the couple's ministry.

One afternoon in 2008 while sitting in my room my cell phone rang, and as I answered I immediately recognized the voice as the same man who spoke to me some years ago in New York. It was the president of Master's International School of Divinity, asking once again if I was ready to take that plunge into their Doctoral program. Although I had come a long way financially, this still seemed unattainable at the time. I remained on the phone a while longer this time, as I found myself telling this complete stranger my life saga. He listened intently and when I was done he told me a story of his own. At the conclusion of that conversation the initial deposit was waived and my monthly fee reduced allowing me the opportunity to register for a Doctoral program in Biblical Counseling/Biblical Studies. I recognized immediately that the toil would be excessive, but I was excited. God had paved the way and I was dumb founded. I started what was supposed to be a three year program, with all the vigor I had when I began my Master's program. This time, however, I would learn about counseling from a Biblical perspective and I was poised and ready to adhere to all that would be taught.

Dating had been placed on the backburner for eight years since my divorce, and suddenly the desire for companionship was playing on my mind. In my opinion I had already been married and God had become my constant companion. As a result of the busyness of life there was never time to even entertain the thought of dating and romance. Although I had recently gone on a couple of casual dates, it was never rigorous enough for me to contemplate anything serious. My Bible doesn't say anything about dating; if I seriously dated it should lead to a commitment, and eventually marriage. I had not entertained the thought of what it would be like to marry someone else. When I married the first time it was for life and therefore any thought of revisiting this lifestyle would have to be implanted in my spirit my Almighty God.

I vividly remember the Sunday morning when I became a member of the church I was attending. I stood beside an unassuming gentleman who I had seen in passing at the church before, but never really took the time to be acquainted with. When the pastor declared us members he asked that we hug the person next to us and it happened to be this person. I thought nothing of it at the time, but this man became constant in my view. As stated previously, it had been years since I even thought about dating, so I chose to ignore all the signs. It was a Sunday afternoon after church as he approached very nonchalantly to ask if I would go for a walk in the park. I was prepared to say no, but when I opened my mouth "yes" came out instead. It was a very interesting Sunday afternoon as I drove up to the park and saw him standing there. I thought it strange that I didn't see him exit a vehicle, but thought nothing of it at the time. As we walked through the park he did most of the talking, as I was still trying to decipher what I was doing there and where this was all going. He told me his unabridged life story which happened to include a six year prison stay. After he said the word prison my brain froze to anything else that he uttered. I went back in time to the sheltered lifestyle that my parents had constructed, and the distance I had travelled on this journey since then. Hence, when he asked if I thought this could go any further I automatically said no. As I was getting in my car, I realized that this man had rode a bicycle and this was his mode of transportation, and my mind stood still once again. As I drove away I wondered what this all meant and in the year to come, although many things occurred, I found myself revisiting that walk in the park.

I watched incessantly as this man rode his bicycle to church Sunday after Sunday and even managed to attend mid-week services no matter what the weather, and I was intrigued at his dedication to the house of God. At times, when I would think about not attending church for no apparent reason, I thought about his allegiance and it gave me the stimulus to go. I remember listening as they announced one Sunday that he had graduated college with his Bachelor's degree. I was very proud of his accomplishment as I knew it was not easy for him to go through all he did and re-claim his life. In essence, it would seem that I was watching as he reaffirmed himself to society and from where I stood it looked like a miraculous achievement. This man who had entered my life that day in the park would persevere in repeatedly asking me about dating, but my answer would always be a polite no thank you, but he was persistent. Because I had been out of the dating venue for so long and had not received any response from God as to whether this would even be a part of my future, I chose to be still.

It was December 2009, my 50th birthday and my daughter planned a great party. Although this man, who will remain, was invited to the party he did not show up. I took this as my cue that there should be no further encounter. The party was great and people came from all over to help me celebrate. I was 50 but God had truly kept me looking pretty fabulous and I was grateful. The Sunday following the party this nameless man gave me a beautiful picture frame and apologized for not coming to the party. The following week I received a beautiful portrait that he painted of me, to which I was really surprised, because I had no idea he was a talented artist. As I looked deeply at the portrait I appreciated the gift and the giver, realizing that while I wasn't paying attention this man had developed real feelings for me. I made the decision that day that if he ever asked again I would go, just so I could get to know him better. I had allowed my sheltered background and the heartbreak of my first marriage to obstruct my vision. However, weeks went by and he never asked again. I received this again as a sign that this was not the plan of God. In 1Corinthians 7:8-9 Paul speaking to the unmarried declared, *"Now to the unmarriedand the widows I say: It is good for them to stay unmarried, as I do. But if they cannot control themselves, they should marry, for it is better to marry than to burn with passion.* This scripture was indelibly fixed in my heart and I knew that if I had to spend the rest of my life as a single person I could do it, and if

God opened the door for marriage I could do that as well. God had a plan and in Matthew 22:14 Jesus said, *"For many are called, but few are chosen"* and I was elated that after all my indiscretions God would count me as part of the few that are chosen. I was ready to do whatever it took to be a soldier in His Kingdom, with all my armor intact. The man in question would eventually ask me out again, and this time, surprisingly to him I would say yes.

Chapter 6

Sweltering Darts for the Children

"In addition to all this, take up the shield of faith, with which you can extinguish all the flaming arrows of the evil one." Ephesians 6:16

My children have always been the force behind everything I have done, and all major accomplishments I have achieved. However, they have also suffered the brunt of separation, divorce, relocation and so much more. I have sometimes wondered as they were growing up if they, at times, desired to be part of another family. I have watched them laugh, cry, and go into seasons of depression and anxiety, as I pressed into God asking Him to deliver them from all residual scars that could hinder their growth and development. In essence, I thank God every day for the only two people who watched, behind the scenes, as I at times fought with everything in me to recapture what the enemy tried to steal. In Ephesians 6:16 Paul explains that the wicked devices of Satan are like sweltering darts. He tries to use these darts to terminate the Christian's faith; but in Proverbs 30 we learn that God is also a defense to those who take shelter in Him. *"Every word of God is flawless; he is a shield to those who take refuge in him. "*(Proverbs 30:5) My children, although raised with Christian values, at times became a pawn in the hands of Satan. I sometimes looked in anguish at the things that occurred in their lives over the years, questioning what I could have done differently to shield them. What would transpire over the years with them required a great exercise in faith. My shield had to be strategically in place, so I could fight the enemy on their behalf and win.

As stated previously in these memoirs my daughter, although seemingly content about our move to Florida, declared her first morning to high school that this was devastating for her. She started her adventure at Port St. Lucie High School, as a result of the address and zoning for my brother's home, where we resided for a short season. She came home daily with a sad look on her face, as if she was totally in despair at the advent of this school. About six months would pass when she finally declared that she had found some friends and the school was not as bad as she expected. Being the social butterfly that she is, she quickly gained her popularity rights, by joining different clubs and participating in events like dance and other extracurricular activities. She soon became acclimated to her surroundings, explaining her hope of not ever having to change schools again. However, when we moved into the home I rented, it happened to be in a different zone. At the end of her tenth grade year I had to deliver the unbearable news that she would once again be changing schools, with only two years of high school remaining. I often speculated as to whether she blamed me for all the changes, and just thought I was absolutely foolish for always uprooting her and her brother.

In August 2007 she started yet another school. Treasure Coast High School, and although the building was brand new, it came with all forms of demons for Shanae. Her choice of friends was frightening for me, as I recognized by their very presence in a room that she had been thrust into a den of wolves. I prayed relentlessly for my daughter, as I watched her change into someone I didn't recognize or even like. She continued actively in the extracurricular activities she had grown accustomed to, but she wore her mask well, camouflaging her double life, just like her mother had done many years before. At times I felt like I was looking at the reflection of what I once was and it hurt to the core. I had unknowingly distributed generational curses to the one I call daughter, and it felt like a knife had been twisted in my gut. I loved her very much, but I didn't like her at all. At times, I felt she hated her brother and me; she would enter the house after her day at school and grunt hello under her breath. Most times, we never saw her again for the rest of the evening and it was fine with us, because her bitterness made the room uncomfortable. Her new found friends and the one she referred to as her "boyfriend" became her family, while her brother and I stood on the sidelines watching in agony.

It was drawing close to Shanae's sweet sixteen. As usual I poured everything into planning a party that would surpass no other. She invited old church friends from Bethel in New York, but her new acquaintances had taken over her life and she seemed completely unaware. I cried out to God on her behalf every day. I had trained my daughter in the way she should go, but from where I stood it seemed like the enemy was winning this battle. Friends came from all over for her sweet sixteen celebration, and although it was a great event, those who knew us well recognized immediately that there was a rift in our relationship, and immediately started to pray. No matter what was going on around me I knew that God would be gracious to my daughter, and she would come forth strong. After that party it seemed like she went from bad to worse, as we fought like cat and dog daily. However, I knew I had to learn how to quench my thoughts, if I was to win my daughter back to God. There was an unforgiving spirit for her dad that had consumed her, and although she denied it I knew she was acting out the years of abandonment and hurt she had experienced. Joel 2:28 states, *"And afterward,I will pour out my Spirit on all people. Your sons and daughters will prophesy"*, therefore, I was looking forward to the afterward for my daughter and believed God that *"no weapon formed against her would prosper."* (Isaiah 54:17)

We had been living in our rented home for almost two years, but I knew in my spirit that God was going to bless us with a home of our own. My children, knowing the financial climate, and how we had lived over the years, did not believe me when I started scouting out the area for the perfect house for us. I felt butterflies in my stomach as I went from house to house in search of the home God would provide for us. I had until May 15th to make a decision to leave our rented home, or try to purchase it at the ridiculous rate being asked. God granted me favor in finding a Christian realtor, who always went the extra mile in helping me acquire an affordable home. When I drove up to 967 SW Connecticut Terrace, I knew immediately that this was the place God had for me and my family. I had been in search of a three bedroom house and God was opening the door for a home with four bedrooms, above what I could ask think or imagine. I believe my children were dumb struck when they saw that this dream was actually becoming a reality. On May 13th I closed on the house, with only a day and a half to vacate our rented premises. There was an overwhelming feeling of joy and fright that welled up in me as I received the key to my own home. God had covered me over the years and performed insurmountable miracles, but nothing compared to this moment. When the time came to pick up the U-Haul truck my son asked inquiringly, who would be driving this massive vehicle? I answered immediately that his mother would. I picked up that truck and drove with tenacity. By the time those who were scheduled to help us move came on the scene, my son and I had packed every item we could carry into the vehicle. The move was complete that same night, and as I was about to lay my head down, I walked through every room declaring and decreeing the scripture I had been given when I lived in the worm infested apartment in Haverstraw New York: Joel 2:25-26, *"And I will restore to you the years that the locust hath eaten, the cankerworm, and the caterpillar, and the palmerworm, my great army which I sent among you. And ye shall eat in plenty, and be satisfied, and praise the name of the LORD your God that hath dealt wondrously with you: and my people shall never be ashamed."* Although the cankerworm was still trying to eat away at my children, God was showing He was strong, and I was excited to be His daughter.

In 2009, one year after moving into our home, I learned that there was something drastically wrong with my neck. The doctors thought that it was as a result of the car accident I had over twenty five years earlier. I suffered excruciating pain, and needed the assistance of my children, in that I found it difficult to even dress myself. Shanae and Jason stepped up to the plate and did everything they knew how to keep me comfortable. When the pain finally became unbearable I decided to have surgery. I chose to have the surgery done to the back of my neck where it was less intrusive and no vertebrae had to be removed. My son had always hated hospitals. However, in April 2009 my daughter, regardless of our differences drove me to the hospital at 5:00 am. I watched her face as they infused me with anesthesia, and although I knew there were many thoughts racing through her mind, she never flinched. She has always managed to exercise great strength, even when life was throwing bitter curves. The surgery was successful and although the recovery was long and painful, I was able to sit on my living room couch to make my daughter a beautiful prom dress. As a result of her chosen lifestyle, friends, and a disobedient spirit, she was one point shy of graduating high school with honors; but I was still determined to make her feel like a princess in her one of a kind designer gown at the prom. The fighting subsided between us, but I knew we did not have the picturesque mother daughter relationship I had hoped for.

When my daughter turned eighteen, our fighting became too much to bear. At her request she left my home, choosing to become the prodigal daughter, and I had no idea where she was living. I recall literally going into my clothes closet, laying on the floor and pouring my heart out to God. I was devastated, not only at the fact that she was gone, but the antagonistic way in which she left. When she was a little girl I remember making her all the best dresses and at times we even dressed alike. She was my princess, and I always knew she would be a phenomenal woman. This episode in our lives was a set back of the enemy, and I had to gain control of my thoughts and release her into the hands of God. I had dreams about her prodigal experience and at times my visions would reveal her in compromising situations. God, however, kept reminding me of the training tools that I had instilled in my children, and always redirected me to Proverbs 22:6, *"Train up a child in the way he/she should go and when they are old they will not depart."* I often wondered how long she would eat the pig slop of the world before finding her way back home, but I never asked any questions, I just waited. It seemed that while Shanae was away our relationship changed, and I believe she grew to appreciate and recognize my love for her. Eventually I received the phone call that I longed for, asking if she could return home. She knew the rules would remain the same, but I also recognized the growth and maturity that had taken place on her prodigal journey, and like the father in Luke 15:11-32, I welcomed her with open arms.

Jason had always been my peaceful child and even when my relationship with Shanae had become estranged, I knew I could always count on my son to exhibit right behavior. I tried never to reveal favoritism with my children, but my son was born with the innate ability to bring healing to all situations. I found myself depending on that as he entered his teenage years. He too was attending Treasure Coast High School and had found what I chose to call the ideal friends, referring to their special group as "PREPP". He was not a perfect child, but his calm demeanor and silly sense of humor always brought stillness to the storms that would continue to rage between my daughter and me. All that came to a standstill when he got to the eleventh grade. He had the same friends, but it seemed like they suddenly became the blind leading the blind. My unassuming son began to exhibit behaviors that were worrisome. I recall thinking I had completely lost my children in the shuffle of life, as the enemy's darts bounced off me and penetrated their very souls. I recognized the symptoms of a child that was consumed by the distractions of this world, but chose to deny in fear. My son the healer was living a lifestyle, which if not quickly quenched, would lead to his spiritual demise.

Although he tried to cover up his behaviors with sarcasm and jokes, it was obvious he was not the same kid. It was obvious that his infatuation with females had entered the picture, and because of his boyish cute looks and debonair smile, he became a pawn in their foolish games. Jason had always managed to hide what he was feeling with his quiet exterior. As a result, all the negative attention always seemed to be lavished on his sister. He allowed his friends to turn him into a somewhat unlikable person that I just could no longer connect with. This was a distressing time for him, as I honestly believe he was sorry for who he had become and couldn't find a way to fix it. His favorite scripture over the years had become *"I can do all things through Christ who gives me strength,"* (Philippians 4:13) but he couldn't seem to get a handle on developing a true lasting relationship with the One who could give him the strength to overcome every obstacle. He was spiraling out of control and his safety net seemed to be bottoming out.

He stayed in his room persistently, and once again I had a child who cherished friends more than family. My heart was broken, but comfort came from my loving Father every morning, as I found my way to my family altar alone to seek His face. *"As the deer pants for streams of water, so my soul pants for you, my God"* (Psalm 42:1) became my signature verse. It seemed like I was breathlessly going after God for my family all the time, and I, at times, questioned if my requests and groans were being heard.

Jason, like his sister graduated High School one point away from an honors diploma. Subsequent to his graduation he took a trip to New York to visit his dad, which he and Shanae had grown accustomed to doing over the years. Upon his return he defiantly announced his desire to relocate back to New York to live with his dad permanently. I often wondered over the years if this might happen one day, but I was definitely caught off guard. My son shut down and in the days prior to him leaving he spoke very few words to me. What a heart wrenching moment this was, and although I tried to remain calm my mind was racing in wonderment of what could have sparked this sudden decision. My son had now become estranged and it was mind boggling. However, I watched in the week to follow as he packed most of his things, got on a plane, and took off for New York. I recall speculating that night when and if I would see my son again, but as I had done in the past I just had to believe God for his safety. The Holy Spirit revealed to me on the day of his birth that he was a healer and a gift from God, and I held on to that promise with the fortitude of a giant.

As I sat in my office some months later I received a phone call from my son. I could hardly recognize his voice behind all the tears. He was so distraught I couldn't find enough words to encourage him. It was obvious that something was very wrong and that this had not turned out to be the trip he anticipated. It turned out to be a three way phone call with him his sister and me, and in hindsight it was actually the day we reconnected as a family. We had become the three musketeers in this war, and seemingly hopeless moments always happened to help us re-group. We managed to bring a sense of calm to Jason that day, and I would call him every day to make sure he was still alright. He came home that Christmas to spend his vacation with me. He had other plans however. It seemed his plans to live with his dad had not worked in his favor, and he begged if he could stay in Florida. I explained that he had made plans with his father and since a round trip ticket was already purchased he would need to go back to New York and plan for Florida in the summer. Plans changed and my son did not get on a plane to New York that morning. He stayed in Florida, but it seemed like he continued to die inside, because none of his dreams were being manifested. My jovial son seemed lost in a sea of depression and I had no idea how to help him. He would refer to Port St. Lucie Florida as the place where young people come for their dreams to die.

In the midst of the turmoil that was escalating in my home I was dating the nameless man on the bycicle. He became the one that would listen to all the woes about my children. He, at times, recognized things as I chose to wear blinders, hoping they would go away. He had become my friend and confidant when it came to certain situations. From the outside looking in it seemed that blessings were being poured out in abundance, and they were, but behind closed doors we had become fragmented by the past. I tried desperately to hide behind ministry, believing one day to recover my losses. God had promised never to leave me alone, but it seemed like my life went from crisis to crisis, as my Job experience continued. I was being afflicted in a new way, but I embraced the fact that *"The righteous person may have many troubles, but the LORD delivers him from them all; he protects all his bones, not one of them will be broken."*(Psalm 34:19-20)

Chapter 7

Gaining Momentum

"Take the helmet of salvation and the sword of the Spirit,
which is the word of God."
Ephesians 6:17

The penning of these memoirs has allotted me the opportunity to share my journey with my readers. As believers we each have a journey that we must travel. The intention of this book is not to cause anyone to think that my passage in this life has been any more rigorous than theirs. The intent is to bring healing and wholeness to the masses, rendering them equipped to fight in their travels and win. In verse 17 of Ephesians 6 Paul reminds us that the knowledge of our salvation in Christ is like a rigid construction hat that defends against the onslaught of Satan. This piece of weaponry covers our heads, the seat of Satan's most massive destruction. Our hard hat helps to solidify our thoughts, turning us to Christ every time for protection. Philippians 4:8 says it best, *"Whatever is true, whatever is noble, whatever is right, whatever is pure, whatever is lovely, whatever is admirable—if anything is excellent or praiseworthy—think about such things."* In verse 17 the warfare journey would not be complete if we didn't hold tight to our sword. God's unadulterated Word is our offensive piece of equipment, that when held tightly enough, can sever and put to death all the forces of darkness that try to defeat us.

My journey has been laborious to say the least, but I managed through every terrain to hold fast to my sword and come forth unscathed. In April of 2010, after a brief courtship, the man I met and walked with in the park almost two years prior, would venture a marriage proposal like no other. It was a Sunday morning service like any other, directly after the church announcements. The pastor had asked me the day before if I would pray, and since that was my favorite thing to do I stepped to the pulpit with no hesitation. As I was about to begin I saw in my peripheral vision as the pastor beckoned to this man. I immediately knew this would no longer be a normal Sunday, but one that would sit in the recesses of my mind forever. Throughout my ten years of singleness I sometimes wondered if I would re-marry. I had become a lone ranger for the Kingdom and was comfortable in my zone. However, I answered yes to that most unusual proposal, and we were married on June 12, 2010. The wedding seemed special, as many came as well-wishers and supporters of this special occasion. It came and went so quickly I hardly had time to breathe, but I recognized immediately that this was different for me. I had become a very strong woman under the protection and direction of my heavenly Father, and I would have to re-adjust my thinking to embrace this man and what he brought to the table.

We honeymooned in Key West, Florida which required a five hour drive and much communication. Although I had watched this man from afar for more than a year before our first date, and had been with him constantly for six months before marriage, there were still some things that confused me about him. This honeymoon would bring everything up close and personal enabling me to see things, that although the norm for many, was very new and different for me. I recall as I watched from the balcony of our hotel room as my new husband lit the biggest cigar I had ever seen, and leaned his head back to enjoy. Those residual habits he had tried to leave in his past were re-surfacing. Although, I believe, this was a pleasurable treat for him it sent shockwaves through my mind, as I immediately realized this may be something I would have to live with for the rest of my life. I sat on the bed questioning myself, as to whether this marriage was a mistake and if so, how I would live with this mistake. It seemed like this honeymoon was doomed for failure, as everyday seemed filled with a new disappointment, removing the excitement of what was to be a thrilling week. On our last evening, it would seem we salvaged the entire week, when we walked up to a hotel and asked an attendant if there was a special restaurant anywhere for us to spend our final evening. He recommended a place called "Latitude". The very name had the sound of something unaffordable, but we decided to take this adventure. The restaurant was on a secluded island and we would travel by boat to get there. We met an interesting pastor and his wife on that boat, as they journeyed to perform a wedding at the restaurant of our choice. Speaking to them was a blessing that evening, as we managed to recoup the devastation of this trip. Although we were told that our seat at the restaurant would not be the best, we were granted favor with the best seat in the house. It was a beautiful ending to what could have been a catastrophe. Although we managed to end our excursion on a positive note, there were still some things that cluttered my mind which we had to address.

The drive home was uneventful and packed with moments of silence. Although this nameless man had always managed to joke his way through many situations, the jokes just seemed to bounce off my mind, as I was deep in thought about the events that just transpired. Weeks would go by as he continued on his smoking binges that made me cringe at times. The smell was nauseating and I was ready to take action concerning this marriage. I knew that God hated divorce, but at times I felt that I would go insane from the smell of cigars and I made the drastic decision to end the marriage. It was during this time that I discovered that we had forgotten to mail our marriage certificate and in the eyes of the court we were not yet legally married. I wondered about this for days, seeking counsel from those I respect in the Christian community. While I pondered what to do I would come home one day to find that my nameless husband had packed his things and made his exit from our extremely short lived marriage. His empty closet was startling, but it also meant I would not have to breathe those cigar smells anymore and that was somewhat comforting. When I reported to a colleague and his wife what had transpired, he urgently invited me to meet with them so we could speak face to face. He uttered many words that evening, but the ones that made inroads into my mind were when he pronounced that "this was not a dating relationship that one could end on a whim, but a marriage where God was present". I already knew that in my spirit, but those words impacted my soul and I made the decision that night to re-acquaint myself with the person I married and fight through the issues that plagued my thoughts. He had moved out, therefore, we would need to re-construct our friendship to journey forward. There were compromises and adjustments that I would need to make to accommodate his habits, and this would be difficult. Though I was not in love, I had grown to love this man in so many ways, therefore, I told God that I would try, and asked Him to equip me with patience and kindness.

Our marriage had faced some obstacles, but we managed to smooth over some of the ragged edges and gain momentum. There are times when I have observed things that brought me to my knees on his behalf, and I am sure if asked he would say the many things he had to alter as well.

The injury to my neck became a thorn in my flesh throughout the years. Three months into the marriage the devastating pain I once felt had returned, this time relieving me of the use of my right arm. This time it would require having major surgery to remove several vertebrae, replacing them with plates and screws. The man I married was exceptional during this time, as he literally walked me through the process. What we had recently experienced paled in comparison to this season, and I thanked God every day that he was there to offer all the help that he lavished on me. Throughout the journey we managed to keep our friendship intact, and even take some memorable vacations along the way. Proverbs 27:17 says, *"As iron sharpens iron, so one person sharpens another"*, and that is precisely what we were doing. I always thought he was a good person, in that after spending six years behind bars, and exiting the prison with only a paper bag in hand, he would go forward to complete a Bachelor's and Master's degree. These were awesome accomplishments and I celebrated his achievements.

My daughter had returned from her prodigal experience with a vibrant desire to serve God. I witnessed as she rose every morning and proceeded to re-establish her relationship with her heavenly Father. Although her connection with her earthly father was still fragmented, she was on a journey of her own that would take her from being victim to victor. She called me every day with new awakenings she had received from God. It was her desire to give back to the kingdom, but this would be a fight, as those young people who remained with the Father while she was gone, like the prodigal's brother, would taunt her every desire to win in her fight. I became her lone cheerleader, as I saw the plan God had for her on the horizon. When she voiced her yearning to launch a ministry called Young Ladies Called to Destiny (YLCTD), I was elated and wanted to help in any way. She tenaciously went forward with this venture endeavoring to start with our youth ministry. Her efforts were almost immediately thwarted by those who called themselves church friends, leaving her with a bitter taste in her mouth concerning church, and those who exalt themselves to a sphere of holiness. In the midst of this fiasco she was asked to present a testimony at one of our youth conferences and although she refused at first, she managed to belt out a testimony, which no one would soon forget. I can vividly recall her baring her soul as the congregation listened in awe. I believe that testimony set her free that night, not only from her past indiscretions, but naysayers that stood in her way. The enemy used the taunting of others to inadvertently lead to a parking lot scene unlike any other with my daughter caught in the middle. She had no fight left in her as far as church was concerned. She was distraught and reverted to distancing herself from the walls of the sophisticated church, endeavoring to re-acquaint herself with her heavenly Father. Although she did not regress to her old ways, she rarely attended our home church anymore.

During this time, I vaguely remember, as Shanae flew through the hallway of our home introducing me to a fair skin young man that she called her friend. I wondered why it was so important for me to meet this person if he was only a friend, but I dismissed it almost immediately. About two weeks later my daughter asked me to go for a walk with her, and I immediately knew something was about to be thrown at me that I might not like. I chose to sit in the front room of the house as she proceeded to tell me about her plans to marry her friend Nick, who I was recently introduced to. This was a curve ball for me, as I had no idea who this young man was. She explained that they would not marry right away, but she had a plane ticket to visit him in California where he was stationed in the Navy and they would be getting engaged. I was glad that I was sitting down, because I think if I wasn't I would have fallen to the ground. I had always braced myself for the unexpected with my daughter, but this was alarming to say the least. Although I was not in agreement with this little rendezvous it seemed all plans were made and I had no say in the matter. Her destination would take her first to New York, where she would encounter an altercation with her dad and then off to California. She was doing it her way and there was nothing anyone could do to stop her. My only reprieve was that it would be a year before she actually married this man and it would give me a chance to get to know him. However, even those plans were about to be altered.

It was a Sunday afternoon like any other about a week after Shanae had taken off for California. I was sitting on the couch preparing to go to a church concert, when a cell phone rang. As usual my Rosie was on the scene for yet another dramatic event in my family, and the ringing cell phone was hers. As she spoke on the phone, and I looked from my peripheral vision, her conversation was very strange and seemed to involve me somehow. When she hung up she spoke with a soft tone, asking me to remain calm, and I knew something strange was about to happen. She calmly let me know that my daughter had posted her marriage to Ian Nicholas II on Facebook. My mouth hung open as I pondered the thought of it all. My daughter was married to someone I had only met once and there was nothing I could do about it. I was dumb struck as I sat still and said absolutely nothing. This was the first time for many years where I could honestly say there was nothing Godly in my mind to say. I couldn't even think of a scripture that would suffice for this moment. I always thought of my daughter's wedding as something that we would happily plan together, and all those plans seemed to be flushed into oblivion at that moment. There were so many different emotions flooding my thoughts, but at the forefront was anger and disappointment. How could she do this? Why would she do this? Who was this young man? The questions were consuming me as I managed to somehow hold back the tears. My daughter kept calling and texting me, but I was unable to answer, as I could not figure out what to say. I knew she wanted to hear congratulations, but all I could think of saying was "are you crazy"? It took a few days before I could answer any of her messages, and I finally did as I sat in my office at work and pondered what had happened. I thought to myself that this might be the biggest mistake she had ever made, but I also thought about different ways in which God could turn this into a miracle. I recall speaking to her in a soft tone as I didn't want to get angry. I needed to speak to this young man, whom I was now supposed to call son in law and I needed to do it immediately. As I walked through Wal-Mart some days later, the phone call came from him, and the first thing he did was apologize for how this all happened. I tried to speak clearly and honestly about my feelings, and all he kept saying was he would never hurt my daughter, and would always take care of her. His voice was sincere, but I also knew that marriage was difficult under normal circumstances, and this was far from normal.

Shanae returned to Florida for a few weeks to pack her things and move to California. Her husband was in the Navy which meant she had chosen a very challenging life and would be spending many lonesome times. I honestly don't think she really understood what this meant, until she actually moved and immediately watched him get on a ship for six months, leaving her to fend for herself across the country in unknown territory. I remember that first phone call, as I listened to my daughter crying, because she had no idea where she was and knew no one. There was nothing I could do but remind her that she had chosen this life and God would protect her. I remember getting off the phone that night and crying uncontrollably for my daughter. Although I was trying to exhibit tough love with her, I could only imagine what she was feeling and my heart just cringed. I immediately went to praying for God to keep her safe and send people along her path that would turn California into home for my child. I took a stroll down memory lane back to when I was nineteen and how unprepared I would have been for such a drastic move. However, she proved herself to be so much stronger than me during those six months, and I realized she was just living up to the meaning of her name.

Shanae went on a rampage to find a church in her new home town. Her husband was still at sea and Sunday after Sunday she would send me text messages about churches she was visiting. She always stated that none of these seemed like home as she continued her search. She received a visit from a friend she had left in Port St. Lucie during this time, whose visit was short lived as a result of certain issues. That visit culminated with the Sunday where she first entered the doors of Open Door Family Worship Center, and a pastor that she would soon call counselor and shepherd. When she called me she stated she had found her home church and a pastor, which she believed, would help propel her back in good standing with her everlasting Father. This was excellent news, as the tone of her voice sparked excitement and hope. She soon became a vital member of this ministry as she joined the dance team seeking to focus her attention on God, using her talent of dance, which was once pronounced dead, as a result of juvenile arthritis. God was allowing her to see that regardless of what was pronounced on her life, He had the power to overrule, establishing that *"no weapon formed against her would prosper."*(Isaiah 54:17)

Jason was also in a tail spin of his own, trying desperately to find himself in the midst of difficult situations. As stated previously, he had always been my peaceful child and even when life hit hard he always managed to remain quiet, though literally dying inside. While he had moved back to Florida with hopes of continuing his education and finding a job, none of those things seemed to be manifesting for him and he looked drained. He spent so much time in his room I became concerned and would check on him constantly. He was always able to camouflage with jokes and laughter, but it was so easy to see the hurt behind it all. The straw that seemed to break the camel's back was the devastating break with someone he confided in. He desperately tried, but seemed to have difficulty getting pass that incident. I prayed constantly that God would help my son, as I knew He had such great plans for him. His favorite scripture had always been *"I can do all things through Christ who gives me strength"* (Philippians 4:13), but he didn't seem to believe it anymore. He also had Jeremiah 29:11 hanging on the wall of his room, declaring *"For I know the plans I have for you declares the Lord, plans to prosper and not to harm you, plans to give you hope and a future."* None of these words were ringing true to Jason at this time, and his choice of friends did not seem to be helping. I recall during that time him showing up, like he sometimes did, to church one Sunday, but instead of sitting in the back he joined me in the front. The message was riveting for him and at the end he fell on his face before the one he calls Father. I thought this might be a breaking point for Jason, but he just couldn't get a handle on what he wanted from this life and just kept on looking despondent.

He always appeared to like technology so I suggested he start attending ITT Tech. We drove forty five minutes to West Palm Beach and he registered for classes, which began almost immediately. It was my desire to see my son succeed and I was poised to do whatever I could to help him do just that. He was attending classes and doing fairly well, but there was always still an emptiness that seemed to hover over him. He spoke very little around the house and there was never any glimmer of joy. My son the healer was in desperate need of healing and all I could do was pray and remind myself that *"from everlasting to everlasting the Lord's love is with those who fear Him and His righteousness with their children's children"*. This scripture brought comfort every time, as I sat and wondered about my son's future. He seemed to like what he was doing in school, but something was still amiss, as he wondered in search of his dream. He was still unable to acquire a part time job and Port St. Lucie seemed like a dead end for my son.

It was during this season that Shanae and her husband expressed their desire for a wedding celebration, and though initially I was still holding on to my disappointment of their initial wedding and wanted no part of it, God allowed me to re-visit 1 Corinthians 13:5 which gives an attribute of love as *"holding no record of wrong"*. As a result of that reminder, I made the decision to plan the best wedding I could with the little I had. Hence, together with my son in law's mother Julie, who had become like family to me, I planned a wedding which was held on August 11, 2012, my children's first wedding anniversary. Many came from all over to celebrate with them and it turned out to be a memorable occasion. It was not just the uniting of my two children, but of two families, solidifying their union in the sight of God and the people who loved Shanae and Nick most. I have to admit that was the day I truly embraced Nick as not just a son-in-law but a son, and I believe new life was also breathed into their marriage on that day.

On the heels of that wedding Jason announced his decision to move to California. His sister had purchased him a one way ticket, allotting him the opportunity to start over in a new place. That was bitter sweet news for me, because even though I knew my son needed a change, I was not ready to release both my children into the arms of a place that seemed so far away. Jason, however, was elated at the thought of a new beginning, which brought comfort to my heart. On September 15, 2012 my son, with a one way ticket in hand, boarded a plane to San Diego California. He was determined to fulfill his purpose scripture which declares *"he can do all things through Christ who gives him strength"*.(Philippians 4:13) I returned home from the airport that day with tears welled up in my eyes, at the advent of my children moving across the country and out of the reach of my hugs. I recall sitting on my son's bed and feeling as though someone had literally died. The grief of that loss seemed unbearable at the time, but I knew it was a positive move for my son and he was in the care of the One that loved him best.

Chapter 8

Applying Weapons for Victory

*"Put on the full armor of God, so that you can take your
stand against the devil's schemes."*
Ephesians 6:11

There is a continuous conflict established in the spiritual realm. It is an individual fight between the flesh and the spirit. It is a social war with the devil, his cohorts, and the evil supernatural rulers that invoke their presence on God's people. In the Old Testament God's people were sequestered for war via the sound of a trumpet. In this spiritual era, a spiritual command is resonating throughout the nations and it is a beckon to a war that cannot be seen with the natural eyes, yet it is a call to strike up the weapons with which we have been equipped. As we re-visit Ephesians 6:11, Paul tells us to clothe ourselves with the whole armor, meaning if there is one piece out of place we have set the stage for an onslaught in which we cannot win. When Paul was writing this portion of his letter to the Ephesians, as a result of his imprisonment he was privy to the Roman soldier in complete armor. He had firsthand knowledge of the weaponry worn during his time, therefore, he used each piece to depict what was necessary for battle if one intended to fight and win. For those living in that time there was a perfect understanding of the imagery, therefore, no question as to what he meant. He describes six pieces of gear used, that when applied, inflicts a lasting blow on the enemy initiating victory for the believer.

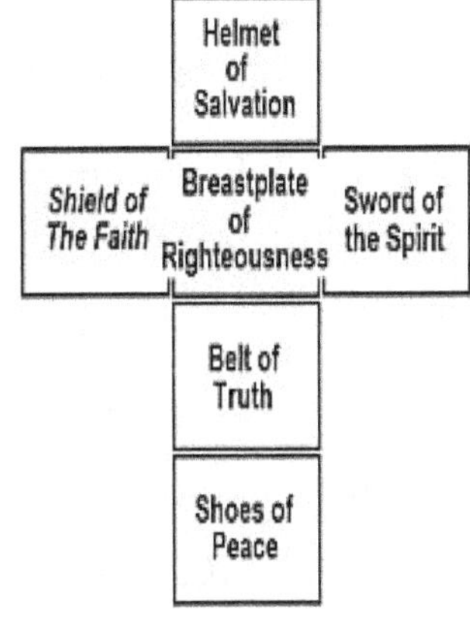

https://www.istockphoto.com/photos/armour-of-god

<u>Belt of Truth</u>: This piece of armor was extremely important, because it was a wide belt worn around the soldiers' waist with loops that allowed him to transport a lot of equipment. This belt was tied in place in several places, so that no matter how the soldier moved, his equipment would remain in place. Hence, if the belt was not strategically put in place everything would be dismantled for the soldier. In the same way that the Roman soldier had to make sure his loin belt was in place every day in an effort to keep his armor together, we as believers must apply God's Word (logos) every day, so we can preserve our resistances. Just as the belt was the first thing the soldier put in place, we too must make this our first line of defense. All the other parts of the arsenal are dependent on the belt being firmly in place. The Word of God is the substance on which our warfare with the enemy is based, therefore, must be put in place daily.

As I reflected on my perfect storm, I realized that the only thing that kept me afloat was the daily spiritual food that I, at times, literally devoured. It sustained and continues to sustain me each and every time. Sometimes when the very breath was knocked out of me, I drew on God's Word, in an effort to regain consciousness. This is a call to my comrades in arm to pick up your own loin belt and feed on it like never before, recognizing the battle is the Lord's and He will defeat all your foes.

Breastplate of Righteousness: The breastplate for the Roman soldier was fastened to the loin belt via leather thongs. It was distributed through rings at the lowest part to keep it securely affixed. It was also attached to the belt and above the belt, making it perfectly clear that the belt had to be put on first. The breastplate, like the name implies, protected the soldier's breast (heart), which is the organ in the body that propels blood through our cardiovascular system keeping us alive. When we are not in right relationship with God, we too, as believers can die spiritually.

When we seek to walk uprightly with God we build a defense against Satan. Matthew 26:41 clearly states, *"Watch and pray so that you will not fall into temptation. The spirit is willing, but the flesh is weak."* Thus, because we are disposed to temptation, we must keep our spiritual eyes open and protect our thought life against the assault of the enemy. As a result of Christ's death and resurrection, we now stand righteous in God's sight.

As I have traveled this remarkable journey, my desire has always been to love what God loves and hate what he hates. This mindset has, at times, made me the minority even among those within the walls of the church. However, I made the decision years ago that I would stand for God even if it meant standing alone. I realize that my salvation is not based on any efforts of my own, however, as a believer, I am *"created in Christ Jesus for good works"*— to assist and serve others. Though there is nothing I can do to earn my salvation, God's purpose is that my salvation will render me a servant in His Kingdom.

Shoes of Peace: All the commentary explanations of the Roman soldier's shoes attribute this to the army's continuous victory. Their footwear had spikes on the bottom, which gave them a firm footing when planted on the ground. This deterred them from losing balance, because the spikes were firmly planted in the ground. The peace of God will help the believer in their stance against the devil. It will assist us when we encounter the harsh places of life, keeping us stable in the face of adversity. Luke 20:42-43 says it best when it declares, *"Sit at my right hand until I make your enemies a footstool for your feet."* Thus, our peace shoes will keep our spiritual enemies under our feet where they belong.

My perfect storm, though accompanied by boisterous winds at times, never swallowed me up because I encroached myself in the bosom of my Savior. Ephesians 4:6-7 gave me the incentive to survive, when at times, I was at my lowest and it states, *"Do not be anxious about anything, but in every situation, by prayer and petition, with thanksgiving, present your requests to God. And the peace of God, which transcends all understanding, will guard your hearts and your minds in Christ Jesus."* There were so many times when I didn't grasp what God was doing, but I chose to take Him at His Word, and it was in those times that my heart was at peace.

<u>Shield of Faith:</u> The shield that the Roman soldiers had was long and covered them from knees to chin. This was to protect them from the arrows and spears that would come at them during war. As a result of the length and width of the shield, the soldier was able to hide behind it in combat. Because it was weighty and awkward, the soldier had to practice to gain flexibility and strength in the use of the shield. At times, soldiers would fight close together holding their shield over head to defend the group from fiery arrows.

In Ephesians 6:16, the Roman shield is a symbol of the faith of the believer. It is not so much about the believer, but about God and the believers' exercise of faith in Him. Hebrews 11:1 says *"Now faith is the substance of things hoped for, the evidence of things not seen."* The believer is called on to exercise faith in an unseen God, for unseen things, and at times, that requires enormous faith. When we know the Bible and have a relationship with the God of the Bible, we are able to exhibit more faith. There is no more amazing security than what we receive from Almighty God.

I have to admit the warzone was intense at times, where I couldn't see the forest for the trees, but God showed up every time. When the forces of darkness came against me, I had to be forceful in putting up my shield regardless of how fiery the enemy's darts were. It is an awesome thing when your back is against the wall, and you are able to watch God become your supernatural shield, defending you on all counts.

<u>Helmet of Salvation:</u> The helmet that the Roman soldier wore was made of the best material known to the ancient world. It came equipped with a chinstrap, and eyeshade, that covered the back and sides of the head. There was also a crest on top that was affixed with feathers, at times, depending on the rank of the officer. The helmet itself was made of bronze (for soldiers), or iron (for officers), and an intricately designed helmet would protect the soldier from all kinds of attacks.

The ultimate battlefield for the enemy is the mind, where he launches his greatest attacks. He wants us to doubt our salvation and uses every tactic to take us to places of despair and guilt. However, we have been given enough arsenals, which if used correctly, will eradicate his attacks, leaving him daunting in his efforts. We must remember that we have control of our thoughts and must take control, if we are to come forth winners. 2Corinthians 10:5 is the assurance for the role we play as it pertains to our thoughts; *"We demolish arguments and every pretension that sets itself up against the knowledge of God, and we take captive every thought to make it obedient to Christ."* We must stay abreast of what infiltrates our minds, realizing our adversary is very subtle and will stop at nothing to render us blind, if we become naive or unthinking believers. Clarity of thoughts is expected, if we are to be perceptive in the situations we must face. This requires daily study of God's Word and constant prayer.

Throughout this pilgrimage I have, at times, had to soak myself in God's Word, in an effort to drown out the lies of the enemy. Satan has been cunning and wicked, but God has been faithful in all venues. I have sought to follow Paul's advice in Philippians 4:8 *"Finally, brothers and sisters, whatever is true, whatever is noble, whatever is right, whatever is pure, whatever is lovely, whatever is admirable—if anything is excellent or praiseworthy—think about such things.* I have had to allow my thought life over the years to endure a complete metamorphosis. What a remarkable journey it has been, when on every path I saw Jesus.

<u>**Sword of the Spirit:**</u> This sword had two edges, and the point was turned upward, in an effort to inflict major damage. It was intended to rip the soldier's enemy to shreds and kill in the process. The sword cut in two directions and was viewed as a weapon of powerful

destruction. Paul emphasizes that the Word of God (rhema), is a potent individual weapon given to the Christian to engage in spiritual warfare.

The believer's sword of the Spirit is a specific Word from God, a rhema individual word. Our ultimate example in wielding this weapon is our Savior Jesus, when He was tempted by Satan in the wilderness. Each Word wreaked havoc on the enemy, ultimately rendering him a defeated foe. As heirs and joint heirs with Christ, we too are expected to employ our weapon of the Word and win on every terrain. When we utter God's unadulterated Word, there is a quaking in the universe that reduces our foes to nothing.

When I contemplate the many times the Word of God has put my enemies to flight, all I can do is rejoice at the advent that I am a daughter of the King of kings. *"For the word of God is alive and active. Sharper than any double-edged sword, it penetrates even to dividing soul and spirit, joints and marrow; it judges the thoughts and attitudes of the heart."* I have the most powerful weapon at my disposal and I will continue to wield it, in an effort to win against the enemy and his demonic forces every time.

<u>**Summary**</u>

Prayer Changes Things

"And pray in the Spirit on all occasions with all kinds of prayers and requests."
Ephesians 6:18a

As I take inventory of this remarkable journey I realize the impact that prayer has had through every crevice of the way. God has been a constant companion, as He entered and continues to enter the atmosphere, at the altar I have built every day, as I meet with Him in my secret place. In Ephesians 6:18, Paul emphasizes the fact that Christians should pray at all times, in all seasons. He also realizes that we should find ourselves in a posture of prayer, even when we don't feel like praying. The Bible declares that we should *"pray without ceasing"* (1Thessalonians 5:17), which means, incessant prayer is crucial to the strength of our relationship with the Lord and our capacity to function in the world. Prayer is to be a lifestyle, and we are to be constantly in a mind-set of prayer. There are a myriad of scriptures that speak to the resolve of prayer and I have listed a few:

- *Be anxious for nothing, but in everything by prayer and supplication with thanksgiving let your requests be made known to God. And the peace of God, which surpasses all comprehension, shall guard your hearts and your minds in Christ Jesus.* (Philippians 4:6-7)

- *The LORD is near to all who call upon Him, to all who call upon Him in truth.* (Psalm 145:18)

- *"And when you pray, you are not to be as the hypocrites; for they love to stand and pray in the synagogues and on the street corners, in order to be seen by men. Truly I say to you, they have their reward in full. "But you, when you pray, go into your inner room, and when you have shut your door, pray to your Father who is in secret, and your Father who sees in secret will repay you."And when you are praying, do not use meaningless repetition, as the Gentiles do, for they suppose that they will be heard for their many words. "Therefore do not be like them; for your Father knows what you need, before you ask Him."Pray, then, in this way: 'Our Father who art in heaven, Hallowed be Thy name.*

'Thy kingdom come. Thy will be done, on earth as it is in heaven. 'Give us this day our daily bread. 'And forgive us our debts, as we also have forgiven our debtors. (Matthew 6:5-12)

- *"And whatever you ask in My name, that will I do, that the Father may be glorified in the Son. "If you ask Me anything in My name, I will do it.* (John 14:13-14)

- *And this is the confidence which we have before Him, that, if we ask anything according to His will, He hears us. And if we know that He hears us in whatever we ask, we know that we have the requests which we have asked from Him.* (1John 5:14-15)

These, and so many others, indicate the importance God places on prayer. This is how the believer dialogues with God, apart from this there is a constant breakdown in communication. Therefore, as a result, my storm has been perfect, because of the times of communication I have established with my Lord. This has been the impetus that has led to the surviving and thriving of my family.

As I scribe this revised version of *Weapons for Victory*, I realize that at the original writing of this manuscript, my daughter had been married and living in California for two and a half years. She announced to me suddenly in October, 2012 that she was pregnant with my first grandchild. Next to the news of me being pregnant with her, this was the best news of my life. Knowing this was going to be a boy child, during the nine months of her pregnancy I prayed that the child in her womb would be a man after God's heart, who would turn his generation towards Almighty God. On June 6, 2013, when I received the news of his birth I realized that throughout this stormy journey God always heard my prayers, and was granting me a blessing that could compare with no other. His name is Ian Martin Alexander Nicholas III and oh what a blessing he is. I traveled to California for the first time, and laid eyes on him four days after his birth and it was love at first sight. I called him my oompa loompa grandson and every time I saw him it brought joy to my heart. I was able to spend five weeks with him after his birth and each morning as I prayed over him I could see a reflection of God in his face. **PRAYER CHANGES THINGS.**

Shanae had grown into the godly young woman that I always thought she would be. She is a wife, a mother, a daughter, a sister, a friend and a mentor. She does each with the tenacity and flare bestowed on her from birth. She went back to school to be a medical assistant and finished the first portion of her studies with straight A's. She was and continues to be a strong brave young woman and I realize now why the name Shanae (God is gracious) Brianna (strong) was so suitable for her. Isaiah 43:1-2 explains *"Do not fear, for I have redeemed you; I have summoned you by name; you are mine. When you pass through the waters, I will be with you; and when you pass through the rivers, they will not sweep over you. When you walk through the fire, you will not be burned; the flames will not set you ablaze."* These verses speak to who my daughter has become even though the enemy has tried to distort the plan of God for her. She has risen to each occasion of Satan's chastisement, only to confirm that he will not win in her life. Though marred by many wounds she stands strong to proclaim to the world *"For the LORD your God is the one who goes with you to fight for you against your enemies to give you victory."* (Deuteronomy 20:4) **PRAYER CHANGES THINGS.**

My daughter bridged the way for her brother to move to California, and embrace a way of life that would allow his dreams to eventually become reality. Though the first few months of Jason's move seemed rocky, he managed to re-group and grow into the gift God has created him to be. He has been allotted the opportunity to enter the walls of a new and lasting church home, attend an excellent school, which as I am writing now, he has graduated from, has a career that will launch him into his future. On my first visit to California I realized the growth and transformation that has taken place in my son, because of his decision to make this major move. He is the embodiment of a young man with a heart for God, and recognizes every day where he would be had it not been for the Lover of his soul. As I watched him Sunday after Sunday, during that visit praising God, it brought tears to my eyes when I thought of the many times the enemy tried to destroy the plan of God. He since, graduated from The Art Institute of California with plans to be a fashion stylist. Who would have thought that my son would have picked up my mantle and be drawn into the world of fashion? John 16:33 says it best when it states *"I have told you these things, so that in me you may have peace. In this world you will have trouble. But take heart! I have overcome the world."* In August 2013 when I received pictures of my son taking the step of water baptism, I was choked up with tears as I thought about his journey.

PRAYER CHANGES THINGS.

I would be remiss if I didn't mention the church, which had embraced my children, thus helping in the recovery of all the enemy tried to steal from them. Open Door Family Worship Center, under the leadership of Pastors Gwen and Charles Matthews became a safe haven for my children, literally saving their lives. My daughter was thrust into the dance ministry, and was given the opportunity to launch Young Ladies Called to Destiny (YLCTD), a ministry birthed out of rebellion and desperation. My son, as stated previously, got baptized and as a result of pastors that care, is walking into his destiny. These two pastors managed to save my children's lives, and so many others that have crossed the threshold into that magnificent edifice. Over the years I have been given opportunities to spend time with Pastor Gwen, and saw in her what branded her a pastor after God's heart. Open Door gave, and continues to give refuge to many, and I pray continued blessing as God uses them to bring revival to San Diego. **PRAYER CHANGES THINGS.**

When I thought about how to conclude these memoirs in 2013, I realized that while I only have one biological sister, our lives had become estranged over the years. I recall when she arrived in New York with her husband and children, how elated my parents were at the thought of their oldest child, and then only grandchildren, truly being a part of their lives after so many years of separation. Our twelve years age difference had always put a rift in our relationship. Though I recognize there are no perfect people, in my eyes my sister Joy, was as close as any could come to being flawless. I believe when God called Israel "the apple of His eyes" He was referring in a special way to my sister. When she and her husband made the decision after a very short stay in New York to relocate to Florida my parents were devastated. I remember watching, as they drove away, and re-entering the house to find my mother sobbing hysterically for her daughter. I knew she loved me, but I also knew there was a special connection between her and her Joy. As I reflected on everything that had transpired over the years since their move, I prayed about how I could re-affirm my relationship with my only biological sister. I called my nieces informing them of my decision to travel to North Carolina where they were currently residing so I could celebrate her. It was a ten-hour drive there, for what I considered one of the greatest Thanksgivings our family had ever encountered. She was never told that I would be coming so the look of surprise on her face when she entered the house to see me sitting in the kitchen of her daughter's home, was one I would not soon forget. As stated previously my parents had three other children that they managed to care for as their own. However, I felt the necessity to re-connect with Joy, seeing that our relationship had become so fragmented over the years, and oh what a celebration it was. As we culminated the weekend my nieces were finally able to share some of the things that had transpired over the years, which laid the foundation for the disconnection of our family. It all made sense now, and I believe that weekend together went on record as the hallmark of a new beginning for all of us. I will treasure the look I saw on my sister's face throughout that memorable weekend for the rest of my life. **PRAYER CHANGES THINGS.**

At the original writing of this book I had been married to the nameless person from the park for exactly three and a half years, and it had been the ride of my life. As stated earlier, our beginning was very rocky, and would become even rockier. The enemy had tried in so many ways to destroy, and though we kept riding the waves the battle would eventually prove devastating. I recognized as I was getting to the culmination of the original writing that this marriage was a mistake on my part, and Satan wanted to use it to take me out. I revised and re-published a book last year called *"Christian Divorce Wars"* and the title speaks to what I encountered in that marriage.

While writing the original manuscript, I found myself in yet another war so I proceeded to pray and ask God for direction. I received counsel and advice from the few with whom I chose to share, but I needed a divine revelation from my heavenly Father. Though I have left New York for almost eight years now, I still considered Bethel Gospel Assembly my church home. Therefore, on a whim as I sat in my office I booked a flight to go home. Once again my friend and confidant Rosie would find herself in the heat of my situation, and as always manage to help readjust my thinking. I was only there for four days, but God had made arrangements to meet me on every venue, which began with our encounter at a women's prayer on that Saturday morning. I had always loved being a part of the Alabaster Women's ministry at Bethel and this was no exception. At the conclusion of that service when asked to lay our burdens at the altar and leave it there, I brought my marriage. On that Sunday morning, while trying to hide in the shadows, I was asked to sit in the front pew with the ministers. God wanted my undivided attention with no distractions. A visiting minister stepped into the pulpit to preach on the topic "Whatever Theology". I sat in amazement as God used her to minister healing to my mind. I was able to re-visit the very words I had managed to pen in the original version of *Christian Divorce Wars*, which stated "marriage is a bond that God has established for life". I realized I had been trying to change the man I married, and even asked God to change him, when in fact the only person I had the power to change was me.

What a revelation it was as I traveled back to Florida with the intention to do whatever it took to stay in an unhappy marriage. Though we managed to be friends,

everything would eventually explode. While writing the
original book, it was my hope that through the thick and
thin of it all the marriage would heal and even bring
wholeness to other marriages. The catastrophic events that
followed would cause that marriage to end, but God would
answer my prayers, by allowing those turn of events to also
be another instrument on my tool belt, which would allow
other marriages to heal. **PRAYER CHANGES THINGS.**

While writing the original book in 2013, it had been
almost fourteen years since the initiation of the divorce war
with my children's father. When this war ensued I
remembered contemplating how this would possibly result
in something good. God had made many promises through
the sword of His Word:

- Psalm 34:19 *"The righteous person may have many
  troubles, but the* LORD *delivers him from them all"*.

- Ephesians 3:20-21 *"Now to him who is able to do
  immeasurably more than all we ask or imagine,
  according to his power that is at work within us,
  ^{21} to him be glory in the church and in Christ Jesus
  throughout all generations, forever and ever!
  Amen."*

- 2 Timothy 4:7-8 *"I have fought the good fight, I have finished the race, I have kept the faith. Now there is in store for me the crown of righteousness, which the Lord, the righteous Judge, will award to me on that day—and not only to me, but also to all who have longed for his appearing."*

- 1 Peter 5:10 *"And the God of all grace, who called you to his eternal glory in Christ, after you have suffered a little while, will himself restore you and make you strong, firm and steadfast."*

In essence He had promised that if I remained faithful like my brother Job, in the midst of my trials and afflictions, I would enjoy His presence in this life and the one to come. The disappointment I experienced when my children's father took flight, set the stage for the divine appointment I would encounter when he made the decision, so many years later, to apologize. I was given the opportunity on several occasions to pray for this man, and the hope was always for his relationship with his First Love to be restored. God's timing is amazing, but when His children choose to pray, trust and believe, He shows up as

Almighty God, everlasting Father and Prince of Peace.
PRAYER CHANGES THINGS.

The journey had been colossal with pitfalls and detours in between, but God had always been the anchor at every juncture expressing His desire for me to come up a little higher. Ephesians 6:10-18 continues to be the framework for this journey, as I recognize throughout that I am in the war of a lifetime, but if I strategically apply my spiritual weaponry I can win on every count.

In October 2012 I once again walked across the stage to accept yet another academic degree. I was ecstatic as the president of Master's International School of Divinity (now Master's International University), conferred on me the title of Doctor in Biblical Counseling/Biblical Studies, graduating with a 4.0 GPA. God had been a constant friend proving Himself on every count to be the Lover of my soul. I owe it all to Him and I take nothing for granted. Through every weakness 2Corinthians 12:9 which states, *"My grace is sufficient for you, for my power is made perfect in weakness." Therefore I will boast all the more gladly about my weaknesses, so that Christ's power may rest on me"*, has been exemplified in me. As a Middle School counselor

I had been able to invest in the lives of my students and help bring healing in so many ways. My counseling practice, Wholeness Counseling Service, was established in 2012, allowing me to meet many people in the community, who placed their lives in my hands, hoping that God would use me, to rescue and bring wholeness to their situations. In November 2012 God also placed in my spirit the desire to start Bridging the Gap Ministry, for a group of young adult women who would meet in my home twice a month. This gave me the opportunity to meet with and minister to some amazing young ladies. I was also given the opportunity to minister and help win and restore souls to the Kingdom via my teaching and preaching ministry. I often reflect on the scriptures I was given as rhema words from God through the years:

Deuteronomy 30:19-20 *"This day I call the heavens and the earth as witnesses against you that I have set before you life and death, blessings and curses. Now choose life, so that you and your children may live and that you may love the LORD your God, listen to his voice, and hold fast to him."* Jeremiah 1:8-10 *"Do not be afraid of them, for I am with you and will rescue you," declares the LORD. Then the*

LORD reached out his hand and touched my mouth and said to me, "I have put my words in your mouth. [10] See, today I appoint you over nations and kingdoms to uproot and tear down, to destroy and overthrow, to build and to plant." These imparted words from the Master placed me in a place where I found myself longing and hoping for a revival in my town. I have attended several churches in Port St. Lucie since then, and been able to bring words of encouragement, utilizing portions of this intense testimony. **PRAYER CHANGES THINGS.**

The Journey Continues

Along this awesome journey I have become preacher, teacher, counselor, author and so many other things, as I sought to answer the call of God on my life. As the war continued and the waters mounted from the surge of the storm, I chose to walk circumspectly with my Savior, and watch as He used me to uproot Satan's territory and bring revival where I was planted.

There have been a lot of changes since I first penned this book. It is my prayer that this revised manuscript will bring healing and restoration to my readers. Take hold of the weaponry bestowed on you by your heavenly Father, and remember it is not like any other weapon. 2Corinthians 10:4 explains, *"The weapons we fight with are not the weapons of the world. On the contrary, they have divine power to demolish strongholds."* You must recognize that no matter what you are going through or have gone through, nothing is too difficult for God to heal. 2 Corinthians 4:7-9 also declares *"But we have this treasure in jars of clay to show that this all-surpassing power is from God and not from us. We are hard pressed on every side, but not crushed; perplexed, but not in despair; persecuted, but not abandoned; struck down, but not destroyed.* God has therefore, provided the entire arsenal you need in His Word, and has made it perfectly clear that, when utilized effectively, the believer will not be demolished. It is henceforth up to you to utilize them and win every battle with the enemy of your soul.

I have revised the original version of *Weapons for Victory: Memoirs of a Perfect Storm* as a transition to the sequel *Armored and Victorious: Memoirs of a Crossover Season.* A lot has certainly happened in the years from 2013 to now, therefore, the sequel is scheduled for release in 2023. What a ride it has been, as I once again utilized the weaponry given in Ephesians 6:10-18. It is my hope that the reader, after digesting this revised work, will be encouraged to read the rest of the story. Truly God has given me the impetus to turn my sour lemons into sweet lemonade, and I pray you are encouraged to do the same. God bless you,

Love Always Dr. Sharon

The Journey Continues

<u>My daughter</u>

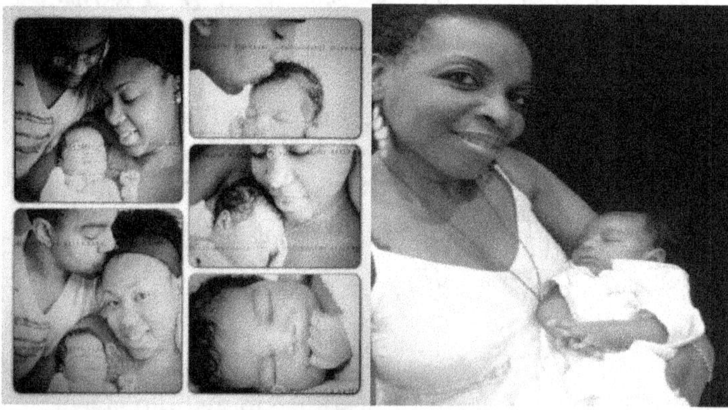

My son

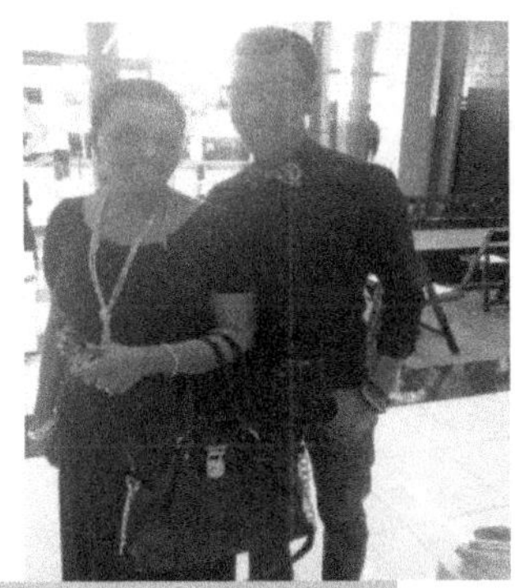

My sister